The Constitution

A Comprehensive Guide to Understanding the Constitution and Its Impact on the United States of America

Written by Douglas M. Rife and Gina Capaldi   Illustrated by Judy Hierstein

Teaching & Learning Company

1204 Buchanan St., P.O. Box 10
Carthage, IL 62321-0010

This book belongs to

_____

Cover photos courtesy of National Archives and Records Administration.

Cover design by Sara King.

Copyright © 2008, Teaching & Learning Company

ISBN 13: 978-1-57310-541-5

ISBN 10: 1-57310-541-4

Printing No. 987654321

Teaching & Learning Company
1204 Buchanan St., P.O. Box 10
Carthage, IL 62321-0010

At the time of publication, every effort was made to insure the accuracy of the information included in this book. However, we cannot guarantee that the agencies and organizations mentioned will continue to operate or to maintain these current locations.

Table of Contents

Dear Teacher or Parent,

Three of the most important words in the Constitution are *We the people*. Those words, which begin our Constitution, turned the eighteenth century world of kings and queens and potentates upside down. Those three words were the harbinger of a New World order where democratic forms of government were taking root, replacing the ancient monarchies of Europe. The power to govern was no longer in the crown of a king but lay with the people, *We the people*.

Though our nation is young among the nations of the world, the United States has the oldest written constitution on Earth. Nearly two-thirds of the world's governments have constitutions drafted since 1970. The American constitution, on the other hand, was drafted in 1787 during a long, hot summer in Philadelphia over 210 years ago. The 55 convention delegates shaped an enduring document that has withstood the test of time. Countries around the world have used it as a model for their own governments.

This book introduces students to the Preamble and the Articles of the Constitution, as well as, the Amendments that followed. Through the activities and games in this book the students will explore why the framers wrote the Constitution in the first place. They will also meet the signers and learn about the arguments and compromises that shaped the document into what has made it arguably the greatest document of its kind.

Students study the Constitution through a variety of activities that test comprehension and understanding of the basic concepts found in the Constitution from the Preamble to the Amendments. The activities and games are designed to work together as one unit but may also be used alone to supplement a textbook. All of these activities can be used to enrich your existing program.

Sincerely,

Douglas M. Rife and Gina Capaldi

Teacher Notes
Constitutional Convention

Objectives

☆ To identify the three main plans put forth at the Constitutional Convention
☆ To identify the events that led to the ratification of the Constitution

Vocabulary

Constitutional Convention   Event at which the framers wrote the document that lays out the foundations of the American government

delegates   The people elected to represent the various states at the Constitutional Convention

Background Information

The Constitutional Convention took place during the summer at Philadelphia, Pennsylvania, in the Old State House. Fifty-five delegates from the former colonies came together to amend the Articles of Confederation. The Articles of Confederation and Perpetual Union was the document that formed the first governing union among the various states. Representatives of the Continental Congress created and proposed the document in 1771, but it was not ratified until 1781. Upon that ratification, the 13 individual former colonies which had become individual independent countries formed the United States of America.

Suggested Lesson Plan

1. Explain the lesson objectives. Review the vocabulary and background information with the students.
2. Invite the students to study the "Constitutional Time Line" handout on page 9 and complete the matching exercise.

Delegates to the Constitutional Convention by State

Indicates delegates who did not sign the Constitution

Connecticut
William Samuel Johnson
Roger Sherman
Oliver Ellsworth*

Delaware
George Read
Gunning Bedford, Jr.
John Dickinson
Richard Bassett
Jacob Broom

Georgia
William Few
Abraham Baldwin
William Houstoun*
William L. Pierce*

Maryland
James McHenry
Daniel of St. Thomas Jenifer
Daniel Carroll
Luther Martin*
John F. Mercer*

Massachusetts
Nathaniel Gorham
Rufus King
Elbridge Gerry*
Caleb Strong*

New Hampshire
John Langdon
Nicholas Gilman

New Jersey
William Livingston
David Brearly
William Paterson
Jonathan Dayton
William C. Houston*

New York
Alexander Hamilton
John Lansing, Jr.*
Robert Yates*

North Carolina
William Blount
Richard Dobbs Spaight
Hugh Williamson
William R. Davie*
Alexander Martin*

Pennsylvania
Benjamin Franklin
Thomas Mifflin
Robert Morris
George Clymer
Thomas FitzSimons
Jared Ingersoll
James Wilson
Gouverneur Morris

South Carolina
John Rutledge
Charles Cotesworth Pinckney
Charles Pinckney
Pierce Butler

Rhode Island
Rhode Island did not
send delegates to the
Constitutional Convention.

Virginia
John Blair
James Madison, Jr.
George Washington
George Mason*
James McClurg*
Edmund J. Randolph*
George Wythe*

Constitutional Convention

1786

Representatives from five states held a convention in Annapolis, Maryland, to discuss problems between the states. Delegates adjourned the meeting deciding little except to plan a convention in Philadelphia the following May to take up issues with all of the states.

1787

The Constitutional Convention in Philadelphia began in May of 1787. Originally the plan was for the delegates to amend the Articles of Confederation, not to propose a new constitution. But on May 25, the delegates voted to write a new constitution. Edmund Randolph of Virginia presented the Virginia Plan. It called for a government with three branches—the executive branch, legislative branch and judicial branch. The legislative branch was to be made up of two houses, both of which would have its number of seats determined by population. The Virginia Plan also proposed that the legislative branch would elect the executive and judicial branches.

The delegates from the smaller states objected to this plan because they believed that the heavily populated states would have too much power. William Paterson of New Jersey offered a nine-point proposal to amend the Articles of Confederation. The New Jersey Plan would have one legislative body, every state having an equal vote. The office of executive was to be led by several people chosen by Congress. Congress would be granted the power to tax and regulate trade. Both proposals were hotly debated at the convention.

Roger Sherman of Connecticut presented the Connecticut Plan. That Plan was a compromise between the two plans and became known as the Great Compromise. It proposed a legislature with two houses, the upper house would have two seats per state, and the lower house representation would be based on population.

After the debates, the document was given to Gouverneur Morris to style. On September 17, 1787, the 39 delegates approved the Constitution. Copies of the Constitution were then sent to each of the 13 states for ratification. Each of the 13 states held conventions to decide on ratification of the Constitution. Delegates in each state were sent to conventions to vote on whether or not their state would ratify or vote for the Constitution to be the new law of the land, replacing the Articles of Confederation. The Constitution was completed and signed in Philadelphia at the Pennsylvania State House and sent to the states for ratification. The framers had debated how amendments could be added to the new Constitution during the May to September convention. There had also been debate about adding a Bill of Rights even before the Constitution was finished.

George Mason of Virginia offered to write a bill of rights. He deeply distrusted powerful, centralized and autocratic government and believed that individual rights had to be protected. Though Mason had authored the Virginia Bill of Rights, the delegates voted down his proposal. Mason was so upset that the document did not include a bill of rights that he refused to sign the completed Constitution.

Below is a chart that shows the dates of ratification, when the vote was taken and what the tallies were for and against for each of the original 13 states.

State	Date	For	Against
Delaware	December 7, 1787	30	0
Pennsylvania	December 12, 1787	46	23
New Jersey	December 18, 1787	38	0
Georgia	January 2, 1788	26	0
Connecticut	January 4, 1788	128	40
Massachusetts	February 6, 1788	187	168
Maryland	April 28, 1788	63	11
South Carolina	May 23, 1788	149	73
New Hampshire*	June 21, 1788	57	47
Virginia	June 25, 1788	89	79
New York	July 26, 1788	30	27
North Carolina	November 21, 1789	195	77
Rhode Island	May 29, 1790	34	32

1788

June 21, the ninth state, New Hampshire ratified the Constitution. The new Constitution went into effect. The new government began to take shape.

1789

April 1, the first House of Representatives was organized.

April 6, George Washington was elected President. He was greeted by cheering crowds from Virginia to New York. Washington was the most celebrated American of his time.

April 30, George Washington was inaugurated as the first President of the United States. He took the oath of office, required by the Constitution, on the balcony of the Federal Building in New York City.

Name _____

Constitutional Time Line

Place the following events in the order in which they happened on the time line below.

☆ George Washington is inaugurated as the first President of the United States.

☆ Delaware becomes the first state to ratify the Constitution.

☆ The Constitution is approved.

☆ The Constitutional Convention convenes in Philadelphia.

☆ New Hampshire becomes the ninth state to ratify the Constitution.

☆ The United States House of Representatives is organized.

Time Line

May 25, 1787 _____

September 17, 1787 _____

December 7, 1787 _____

June 21, 1788 _____

April 1, 1789 _____

April 30, 1789 _____

Constitution Mini Book

Objective

☆ Students will make a sample copy of the Constitution. They will do this by incorporating the Preamble, Bill of Rights, Articles and Amendments found within the pages of this book. The *Constitution Mini Book* may be used as a handy study guide for individuals or groups.

Background Information

The Constitution is the supreme law of the United States of America. It provides the framework for the government; outlines the three main branches of the government; outlines which powers each branch may exercise; reserves the rights for individuals, states and the federal government.

Materials

white thread	water	8½" x 11" white paper
sewing needle	paper towels	ruler
black tea	shallow pan	utility knife

Directions

1. Reduce and copy the pages of the Constitution, Preamble, Bill of Rights, Amendments, etc., within this book so that two pages fit on an 8½" x11" sheet of paper.
2. Brew tea and allow to cool. Pour into the shallow pan.
3. Add two additional blank sheets of paper and place one top of the reduced copies. Slip each page into the shallow pan to stain it for a moment or two. Pull the paper out quickly and lay flat. Place a paper towel between each sheet. Lay a heavy object, such as a telephone book on the pile of drying papers and let dry. (Figure 1)
4. Fold each sheet in half and place in numerical order. Keep two plain sheets first in the book. (Figure 2)
5. Sew the folded sheets together with simple running stitches. (Figure 3)
6. Decorate the cover of the Constitution book and use for easy reference. Illustrate the various blank pages to represent the text.

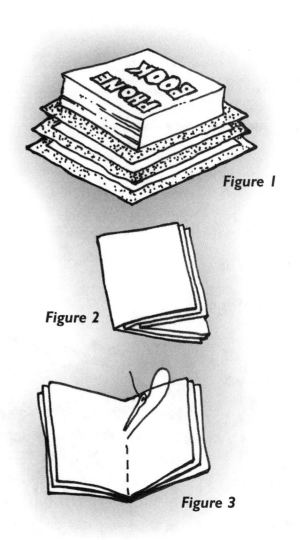

Figure 1

Figure 2

Figure 3

Teacher Notes
Constitutional Convention

Objectives
☆ To understand the excitement of the Constitutional Convention at the time
☆ Be able to interpret the lyrics of the song
☆ To understand the song as propaganda
☆ Identify propaganda techniques

Vocabulary

Columbia   The female figure symbolizing the United States

palladium   A palladium is anything meant to ensure or safeguard something else, in this case, the safeguard to the United States. According to the song title, "The Grand Constitution: Or, the Palladium of Columbia: A New Federal Song," a nearly perfect translation is that the Constitution is a safeguard (Palladium) of the United States (Columbia).

muses   According to Greek mythology, there were nine daughters of Zeus considered to be goddesses or muses. These nine goddesses inspired the creative process. The nine muses are: Calliope the muse of epic poetry, Clio the muse of history, Erato the muse of the poetry of love, Euterpe the muse of music, Melpomene the muse of tragedy, Polyhymnia the muse of sacred poetry, Terpsichore the muse of dance, Thalia the muse of comedy and Urania the muse of astronomy.

Kamschatka   The large peninsula between Siberia and China.

commonweal   The archaic meaning is "Commonwealth." In the context of the song, the writers are referring to the American republic.

Republican   A person who believes in a form of government where the ultimate power lies with the voters and the representatives in which they, by voting, invest power in them to govern.

Shays   The song says to "Shays and Days dare not to rebel." The Shays refers to Daniel Shays, a 39-year-old Massachusetts farmer who led a rebellion against the nascent government he had fought valiantly for in the American Revolution. The rebels who were suffering from high debts and high taxation were trying to close down the debtor's prison and receive some relief from the state government. The rebellion which began in late August of 1786, culminated in an attack against a Federal arsenal at Springfield on February 3, 1787. The long-term effect of the rebellion was a call for a stronger national government.

Days	The "Days" in the song refers to Luke Day, who was a compatriot of Daniel Shays
huzza	A cheer, such as, "hurrah!"

Propaganda Techniques

bandwagon	In this type of propaganda technique the propagandist wants the viewer or listener to believe that everyone is using the products or that everyone believes in this particular thing.
endorsements	In this form of propaganda a well-known and popular person, such as a famous basketball player, is used to endorse a concept or product, perhaps giving a testimonial that he only wears a certain brand of basketball shoe.
glittering generalities	This propaganda technique uses sparkling words, positive phrases, and glowing adjectives to paint the most positive image for the viewer or reader.

Background Information

The song, "The Grand Constitution: Or, the Palladium of Columbia: A New Federal Song," appeared in the *Massachusetts Centinel* on October 6, 1787, only weeks after the Constitutional Convention had concluded. The Federalists, those who were in favor of the ratification of the Constitution, and the Anti-Federalists, who were opposed to ratification, debated the merits of the passage of the Constitution throughout the 13 former British colonies. Proponents on both sides used many formats in newspapers, such as editorials and songs, to sway readers during the ratification debate.

Suggested Lesson Plan

1. Explain the lesson objectives. Review the vocabulary and background information.
2. Read and discuss the song with the class.
3. Invite students to answer the questions about the song in the handouts on pages 15–16.
4. Invite students to find examples of these three types of propaganda in the newspaper.

The Grand Constitution:
Or, the Palladium of Columbia:
A New Federal Song

[1] From scenes of affliction—Columbia opprest—
Of credit expiring—and commerce distrest,
Of nothing to do—and nothing to pay—
From such dismal scenes let us hasten away.
> *Our Freedom we've won, and the prize let's maintain*
> *Our hearts are all right—*
> *Unite, Boys, Unite,*
> *And our Empire in glory shall ever remain.*

[2] The Muses no longer the cypress shall wear—
For we turn our glad eyes to a prospect more fair:
The soldier return'd to his small cultur'd farm,
Enjoys the reward of his conquering arm.
> *"Our Freedom we've won."* &c.

[3] Our trade and our commerce shall reach far and wide,
And riches and honour flow in with each tide.
Kamschatka and *China* with wonder shall stare,
That the *Federal* Stripes should wave gracefully there.
> *"Our Freedom we've won."* &c.

[4] With gratitude let us acknowledge the worth,
Of what the CONVENTION has call'd into birth,
And the Continent wisely confirm what is done
By FRANKLIN, the sage, and by brave WASHINGTON.
> *"Our Freedom we've won."* &c.

[5] The wise Constitution let's truly revere,
It points out the course of our EMPIRE to steer,
For oceans of bliss do they hoist the broad sail,
And peace is the current, and plenty the gale.
   "Our Freedom we've won." &c.

[6] With gratitude fill'd—let the great Commonweal
Pass round the full glass to Republican zeal—
From ruin—their judgment and wisdom well aim'd,
Our liberty, laws, and our credit reclaim'd.
   "Our Freedom we've won." &c.

[7] Here Plenty and Order and Freedom shall dwell,
And your Shays and Dayes won't dare to rebel—
Independence and culture shall graciously smile,
And the Husbandman reap the full fruit of his toil.
   "Our Freedom we've won." &c.

[8] That these are the blessings, Columbia knows—
The blessings the Fed'ral CONVENTION bestows.
O! then let the People confirm what is done
By FRANKLIN the sage, and by brave WASHINGTON.
   Our Freedom we've won, and the prize we'll maintain
      By jove we'll Unite,
      Approve and Unite—
   And huzza for Convention again and again.

Name _____

The Grand Constitution;
Or, the Palladium of Columbia;
A New Federal Song

1. In the first stanza, how does the song describe the state of America prior to winning its

    freedom? _____

2. From whom did the Americans win their freedom? _____

3. In the first stanza, what does the song suggest will guarantee freedom? _____

    _____

4. In the second stanza, who did the Muses refer? _____

    _____

5. In the second stanza, what are the soldiers doing after the war? _____

    _____

6. In the third stanza, what is gained by winning freedom? _____

    _____

7. In the fourth and eighth stanzas, why does the lyricist mention Franklin and Washington?

   _____

8. Which propaganda technique is being used with the mention of Franklin and Washington—
   bandwagon appeal, endorsement or glittering generalities? Explain your answer.

   _____

9. Who are Shays and Days? _____

   _____

10. In the seventh and eighth stanzas, what does the song indicate are the blessings that the

    Convention will bestow? _____

    _____

11. Which propaganda technique is being used in the seventh and eighth stanzas—bandwagon
    appeal, endorsement or glittering generalities? Explain your answer. _____

    _____

    _____

12. Songs were used as part of the debate between factions in favor and factions opposing the
    Constitution. Is the lyricist for the passage of the Constitution by the states or opposed to
    the passage? Explain your answer using quotes from the song to support your answer.

    _____

    _____

Constitution Road Trip Board Game

Objective
☆ To understand the time frame and logistics the delegates faced in order to write the Constitution.

Background Information
In this game, each player represents a congressional delegate who has been chosen by his or her state to write the country's first Constitution. The game board represents the city of Philadelphia in which most of the delegates gathered for the first and second congressional meetings. To win, a student must earn a minimum of five Liberty Bell tokens and reach the finish.

*Up to five students

Optional
Game is based on the text within this chapter. Incorporating additional chapters is appropriate.

Materials
die	Washington nickel for each player	tag or poster board
cardboard	pencil	spray glue
paper		

Directions

1. Copy the game board on pages 18-19 and mount on tag or poster board.
2. Reproduce five Liberty Bell tokens from page 20 for each player.
3. Explain game rules to players. Pass around one nickel for each student to use as a marker and begin play.
4. The first player rolls the die and moves a Washington nickel to a designated square.
5. The player reads the description for the square in the Constitution Road Trip Board panel found in the middle of the game board. Instructions for each square are described.
6. The die is passed to the next player and play resumes.

Rules

☆ Determine which player will go first. Distribute one nickel for each player to use as a token.

☆ If a player lands on the square "Caught by British Army for Treason, land in jail" the only way to get out is to roll a 5, then move ahead five spaces. If a player rolls an even number, he or she must wait a turn, then try again.

☆ If a player lands on a square that asks for a Liberty Bell token, but has none, the game continues.

☆ The Start/Finish box is only significant to the player who begins the game or is moving to finish the game.

☆ Players must keep track of their wins and losses on a piece of paper.

☆ To win, players must collect five Liberty Bell tokens and continue playing until they reach the Finish box.

☆ A player does not need the exact number to reach the Finish box and end the game.

Start/Finish 1

2

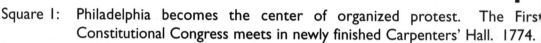

3

4

22

Constitution Road Trip

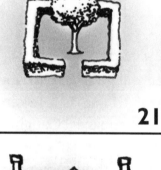

21

20

Square 1: Philadelphia becomes the center of organized protest. The First Constitutional Congress meets in newly finished Carpenters' Hall. 1774.

Square 2: Warfare begins in Massachusetts; Congress creates Army—appoints George Washington as Commander in Chief.

Square 3: Declaration of Independence adopted on July 4, 1776. Four days later it is publicly read to the citizens in Philadelphia. Move ahead three spaces.

Square 4: August 2, 1776. Formal signing of the Declaration of Independence with 56 signers…others sign later. One Liberty Bell token taken.

Square 5: Caught by British Army for Treason, land in jail.

Square 6: Constitutional Convention holds secret session in Independence Hall. Earn two Liberty Bell tokens.

Square 7: Articles of Confederation adopted in 1777, giving Congress only limited power. Congress is unable to regulate domestic affairs, no power to tax regulate power or commerce. There is no money to pay soldiers for their service in the Revolutionary War. Move ahead four spaces.

Square 8: Troubles with Confederation of States. Southern states battle northern states for economic advantage. Congress does not have power to change situation. Lose one turn.

Square 9: Congress stays in Philadelphia until 1783. Earn one Liberty Bell token.

Square 10: 1786, United States is bankrupt. Congress does not have power to change situation. Lose one Liberty Bell token.

Square 11: Caught by British Army for Treason, land in jail.

Square 12: Troubles with Confederation of States: Americans are thought of as a "third rate republic." Congress does not have power to change situation. Lose one turn.

19

18

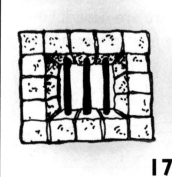

17

16

18

 **5**

 **6**

 **7**

 **8**

Board (Philadelphia)

 **9**

Square 13: Angry farmers in Massachusetts take up arms with Daniel Shays in order to gain debt relief. Congress does not have power to change situation. Lose one Liberty Bell token.

Square 14: A second Continental Congress is called. Delegates meet in Philadelphia to make provisions in the Constitution. Provisions give Congress more power for a stronger government. Move ahead four spaces.

Square 15: Independence Hall/Pennsylvania State House. Second Constitutional Convention begins in May 25, 1787. Delegates from states meet to debate the proposed Constitution. George Washington is elected president of the Convention. Add one Liberty Bell token.

Square 16: New structure of government grants Congress the ability to regulate the economy, currency and national defense. Turn back four spaces.

Square 17: Caught by British Army for Treason, land in jail.

Square 18: Thirty-nine of fifty-five delegates support the new Constitution. (Rhode Island opposes the Convention—sends no delegates.) Earn two Liberty Bell tokens.

Square 19: After signing the Constitution on September 17, delegates dine together at the City Tavern. Lose one Liberty Bell token.

Square 20: Congress meets in County Courthouse (Congress Hall). Earn one Liberty Bell token.

Square 21: George Washington inaugurated for second term as President, 1793. Earn three Liberty Bell tokens.

Square 22: John Adams inaugurated as second President in 1797. Sworn in at Congress Hall Senate chambers.

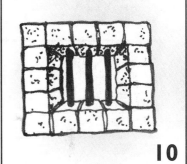 **10**

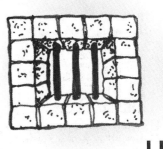 **11**

 **15**

 **14**

 **13**

 **12**

Liberty Bell Tokens

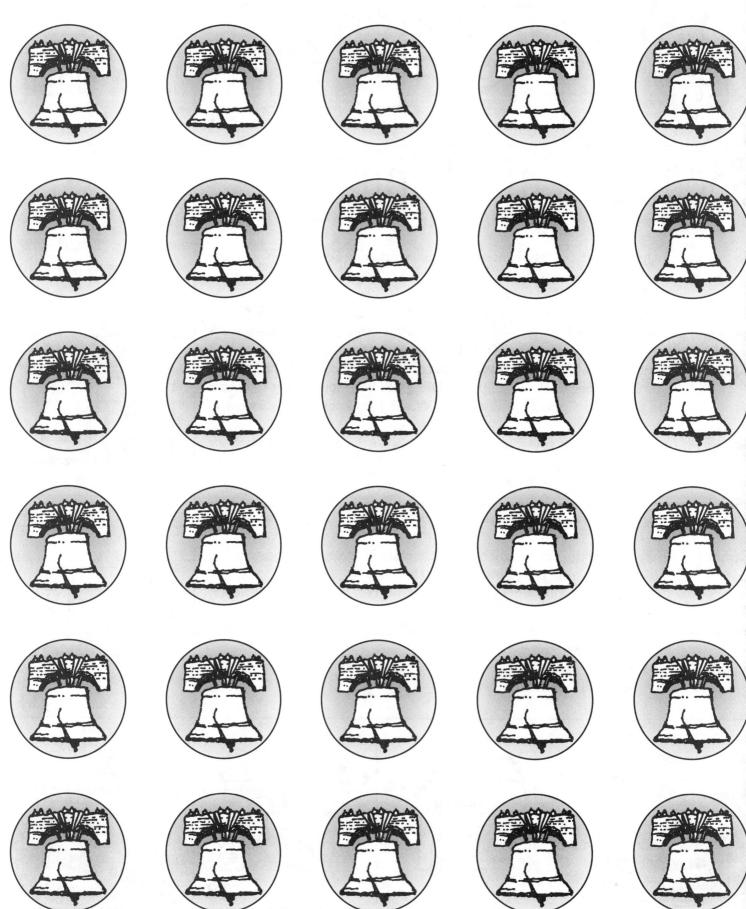

Teacher Notes
The Preamble

Objectives

☆ To understand the importance of the Preamble
☆ To be able to restate the reasons the Constitution was written

Vocabulary

more perfect union	A better government
establish justice	Set up a court system whereby the citizens would be assured their rights and liberties but could settle civil matters and criminal matters with fairness and impartiality
domestic tranquility	The ability to keep the peace
common defense	The government's ability to defend the county and the people against foreign invasions or enemies.
general welfare	People's health and happiness. This means something entirely different today.
posterity	Future generations

Background Information

The Preamble of the United States Constitution is one sentence long, but lays out two very important concepts. First the Preamble starts with *We the people* clearly stating that the people of the country are the sovereigns or the rulers. The implication here is that "we the people" is not a king or a monarch or God, from which the authority is derived. This is a compact or a contract between the government and the governed.

The second concept that is embedded in the Preamble is the reasoning behind why the framers wrote the Constitution.

"We the people of the United States, in order to form a more perfect Union, establish justice, insure domestic tranquility, provide for the common defense, promote the general welfare, and secure the blessings of liberty to ourselves and our posterity, do ordain and establish this Constitution for the United States of America."

The preamble lays out the six reasons for the Constitution:

...to form a more perfect Union...

The United States had been governed by a loose confederation of states in a document called the Articles of Confederation, in effect in 1777 and ratified in 1781. But under the Articles of Confederation there was no strong central government which made it difficult for the states to act in unison. The men who came together in May of 1787 to "fix" the Articles of Confederation gave that up to re-write it entirely. Their intent was to create a more perfect union.

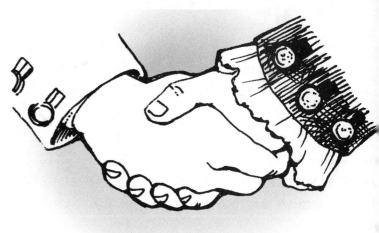

...insure domestic tranquility...

During the Shays Rebellion, the various states could not agree on how to provide for the troops to put down the rebellion. The Articles of Confederation did not provide for a standing army or the ability of the government to raise taxes or charge tariffs to pay for such an army. Because the Articles were weak, Massachusetts was left on its own to put down the rebellion. Eventually some of the money to pay for the troops to stop Shays, Day and the others was raised by some of the merchants and business people being threatened by the rebels. Over four thousand troops led by General Benjamin Lincoln put down the rebellion but leaders in all of the colonies saw the exposed weakness of the Articles of Confederation.

...establish justice...

There were many penalties and injustices that the framers wanted to do away with when they wrote the Constitution. The memories of the laws and the special courts of the King were also fresh. Of the 55 men who came to the convention, only 39 signed the document. Some refused to sign because there was no Bill of Rights guaranteeing certain freedoms.

...provide for the common defense...

The collective states of the United States had just fought a war with Great Britain, the greatest military power of the Western world at that time. The framers were under no illusions that they may well be called upon to defend America again, and they would need the government to have the ability to raise and pay for an army and a navy if necessary.

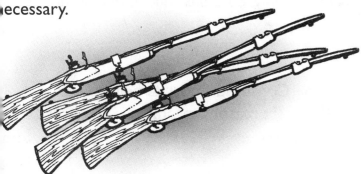

...promote the general welfare...

This clause refers to the government's ability to create a country so every state and every citizen could benefit from the collective good that could be produced by a strong and powerful government—expansion of trade, the growth of the nation, fairness of laws and safety for industry and investment.

...secure the blessings of liberty to ourselves and our posterity...

The framers were intent on forming a government that would safeguard the liberty and freedoms that had been so hard fought only a few years earlier. They also wanted to make sure that the government would provide liberty for their children and grandchildren.

Suggested Lesson Plan

1. Explain the lesson objectives. Review the vocabulary and background information with the class.
2. Read and discuss the Preamble with the class.
3. Invite students to answer the questions in "The Preamble" handout on page 24.
4. The handouts on pages 25-30 pertain to government agencies and acts and how they relate to various stated reasons in the Preamble of the Constitution.

Name _____

The Preamble

We the people of the United States, in order to form a more perfect Union, establish justice, insure domestic tranquility, provide for the common defense, promote the general welfare, and secure the blessings of liberty to ourselves and our posterity, do ordain and establish this Constitution for the United States of America.

List the six reasons contained in the Preamble to the Constitution for its being written. Explain in your own words what those six reasons mean.

1. _____

2. _____

3. _____

4. _____

5. _____

6. _____

The Preamble

We the people of the United States, in order to form a more perfect Union, establish justice, insure domestic tranquility, provide for the common defense, promote the general welfare, and secure the blessings of liberty to ourselves and our posterity, do ordain and establish this Constitution for the United States of America.

"in order to form a more perfect Union,..."

Read the phrase excerpted from the Preamble.
Circle the governmental institutions and acts that best relate to the phrase.

A. The **Thirteenth Amendment** was ratified December 18, 1865, and banned slavery in the United States.

B. The **National Security Council** advises the President on issues that threaten the United States.

C. The **United States Air Force** was created.

D. The **Nineteenth Amendment** of the Constitution, ratified on August 18, 1920, guarantees women the right to vote.

E. The **Cooperative Extension** was established in 1914 to deliver the most up-to-date agricultural information to the nation's farmers.

F. In 1933, the **Tennessee Valley Authority** was created to develop a series of dams to tame the tributaries and the Tennessee River and provide hydroelectric power.

G. The **Fourteenth Amendment** was ratified on July 28, 1868, and guaranteed that all citizens born or naturalized would have all rights of every other citizen no matter their race, that every citizen was guaranteed due process of law and equal protection of the law.

H. The first 10 Amendments to the Constitution, known as the Bill of Rights, went into effect on December 15, 1791. These 10 Amendments protect the most fundamental American freedoms.

Name _____

The Preamble

We the people of the United States, in order to form a more perfect Union, establish justice, insure domestic tranquility, provide for the common defense, promote the general welfare, and secure the blessings of liberty to ourselves and our posterity, do ordain and establish this Constitution for the United States of America.

"establish justice,..."

Read the phrase excerpted from the Preamble.
Circle the governmental institutions and acts that best relate to the phrase.

A. The **Department of Justice** was established by an act of Congress, signed into law by President Ulysses S. Grant on June 22, 1870.

B. Congress established **Headstart** in 1966 to give children quality preschool.

C. The **Department of Homeland Security** was formed November 25, 2002.

D. The **Judiciary Act of 1789**, adopted on September 24, 1789, by the first Congress, established the Supreme Court and the federal court system.

E. The **National Endowment for the Arts**, created in 1965, funds community art programs such as theater, artists' shows and art education.

F. In 1789, George Washington appointed Edmund Jennings Randolph as the first Attorney General.

G. The first Supreme Court Chief Justice, John Jay, was nominated by George Washington in 1789.

H. The **Corporation for Public Broadcasting** was established by an act of Congress in 1967.

Name _____

The Preamble

We the people of the United States, in order to form a more perfect Union, establish justice, insure domestic tranquility, provide for the common defense, promote the general welfare, and secure the blessings of liberty to ourselves and our posterity, do ordain and establish this Constitution for the United States of America.

"insure domestic tranquility,..."

Read the phrase excerpted from the Preamble.
Circle the governmental institutions and acts that best relate to the phrase.

A. President Abraham Lincoln enacted the **Emancipation Proclamation** in 1863, freeing slaves in the Southern states.

B. The **Federal Housing Administration** was established as a way to aid families buying homes.

C. Congress passed the **Clean Air Act** in 1970 to reduce pollutants from being released into the air.

D. The **National Defense Act** of 1947 established the Air National Guard.

E. After reading Upton Sinclair's book, *The Jungle*, about the meat packing industry, President Theodore Roosevelt pushed Congress to establish the **Food and Drug Administration**. The mission of the FDA is to insure the cleanliness and safety of the county's food supply.

F. The Mississippi National Guard units were activated by the governor of the state to provide aid after landfall was made by Hurricane Katrina in 2005.

G. The United States governor passed the **G.I. Bill** in 1944 to provide financial support for the returning World War II soldiers who wanted to get a college education.

H. The **Navy Department** was founded in 1798.

The Preamble

We the people of the United States, in order to form a more perfect Union, establish justice, insure domestic tranquility, provide for the common defense, promote the general welfare, and secure the blessings of liberty to ourselves and our posterity, do ordain and establish this Constitution for the United States of America.

"provide for the common defense,..."

Read the phrase excerpted from the Preamble.
Circle the governmental institutions and acts that best relate to the phrase.

A. The National Guard was created when Congress passed the Militia Act of 1903. This act organized all of the state militias into the current National Guard system.

B. Congress passed the **Truth in Packaging Act** in the 1960s to aid consumers in their buying choices.

C. The **Central Intelligence Agency** was formed to gather information from parts of the world to insure the safety of American security forces.

D. The **Department of War** was established in 1789 which later became the **Department of Defense**.

E. Congress established **Medicaid** in 1965 to provide medical care to the poor and the elderly.

F. The **Coast Guard** was established January 28, 1915, as another branch of the United States military.

G. The **Environmental Protection Agency** was created to clean up toxic waste dumps and to protect the United States' environment.

H. The **Manhattan Project** was the secret project with scientists from the United States, Canada and the United Kingdom to develop a nuclear weapon, directed by Robert Oppenheimer from 1941-1946.

The Preamble

We the people of the United States, in order to form a more perfect Union, establish justice, insure domestic tranquility, provide for the common defense, promote the general welfare, and secure the blessings of liberty to ourselves and our posterity, do ordain and establish this Constitution for the United States of America.

"promote the general welfare,..."

Read the phrase excerpted from the Preamble.
Circle the governmental institutions and acts that best relate to the phrase.

A. The **State Children's Health Insurance Program (SCHIP)** was enacted into law by the United States Congress in 1997 to help states provide health insurance for poor children.

B. Congress enacted **VISTA**, a community action program, in the mid-1960s. The acronym stood for Volunteers In Service To America.

C. The **Marshall Plan** was developed to supply economic aid to the war-torn countries of Western Europe after World War II.

D. The United States **Department of Education** was formed October 17, 1979, while Jimmy Carter was President.

E. The **United Nations** was founded in 1945 after the end of World War II. The United States was one of the charter, or founding, members.

F. The **National School Lunch Program (NSLP)** was designed to provide schools with nutritious lunches either at a low cost or free to school children in need.

G. The United States became a signatory of the **North Atlantic Treaty Organization (NATO)** on April 4, 1949.

H. In the **Higher Education Act** of 1965, grants of money were created to help college-age students pay for college. The grants are now known as Pell Grants, named after United States Senator Claiborne Pell from Rhode Island.

The Preamble

We the people of the United States, in order to form a more perfect Union, establish justice, insure domestic tranquility, provide for the common defense, promote the general welfare, and secure the blessings of liberty to ourselves and our posterity, do ordain and establish this Constitution for the United States of America.

"and secure the blessings of liberty to ourselves and our posterity,..."

Read the phrase excerpted from the Preamble.
Circle the governmental institutions and acts that best relate to the phrase.

A. The **Voting Rights Act** of 1965 assured that all citizens regardless of color could vote. This law struck down poll taxes that had been used to prevent African Americans from voting in the South.

B. Established in 1910, **Glacier National Park** in Montana covers 16,000 square miles.

C. The **Fish and Wildlife Service** was formed in 1940 to protect and manage wildlife for the benefit of all Americans.

D. In 1792, the United States began minting coins.

E. **Yellowstone National Park**, home of Old Faithful, the most famous site in the park, became the world's first national park on March 1, 1872.

F. The **National Weather Service** was established in 1890 to provide weather information to sailors, farmers and aircraft pilots.

G. The **National Park Service** was created in 1916 to preserve some of the most beautiful areas in America.

H. The **Endangered Species Act**, passed by Congress in 1973, was designed to protect plant and animal species on the verge of extinction, as well as, the ecosystem in which they live.

☆☆☆ Re-Creating the Preamble ☆☆☆

Objective

☆ Students will re-create the Preamble to the Constitution for a more meaningful experience. They will do this by incorporating old style writing techniques with a goose quill pen.

Background Information

The Preamble to the United States Constitution is a brief statement which describes the purpose and principles that the Constitution was meant to serve. It expresses the author's intentions and what the Constitution meant and hoped to achieve.

Optional

This project may also be incorporated in the overall Constitution book by using old style techniques as seen in the activity to make a *Constitution Mini Book* (page 10).

Individual or group project

Materials

large feather—goose, turkey, crow, found in craft stores
X-acto™ blade or utility knife
newspapers for blotting
½" x 11" white paper
bowl of warm water
India ink
safety pins
masking tape
black tea bag
shallow pan
pencil

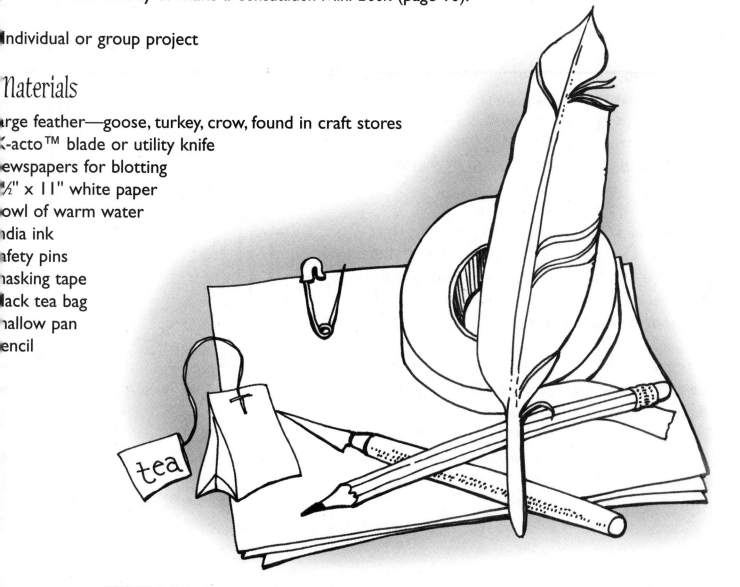

Directions

1. Students will choose a signer of the Constitution and research his signature.

2. To make the quill pen, pull away four inches of the downy feathers from the base of the quill. (Figure 1)

3. Soak the quill in warm water. Slice the quill on one side in a slant. Follow the same procedure on the other side to make a point. Cut a small ¼" slit in the middle of the quill to make a point. (Figure 2)

4. Use a pin to pull the matter from the inside of the hollow quill. (Figure 3)

5. Copy the sample of the Preamble (page 33).

6. Stain a blank sheet of paper with tea by allowing it to soak in a shallow pan. Pull out once you see that the paper color is stained and blot between paper towels. Place a heavy object on the paper and allow to dry, wrinkle free.

7. Tape the facsimile sample of the Preamble to a window. Lay the stained paper onto the Preamble and follow the scripted letters with light pencil lines. Include the name of the researched signer. (Figure 4)

8. Practice writing the Founding Father's signature on a blank sheet of paper. Do this by first dipping the quill point into the ink. Blot the point on paper towels so it will not drip. Follow the pencil lines to create your own copy of the Preamble and signature of a Founding Father. (Figure 5)

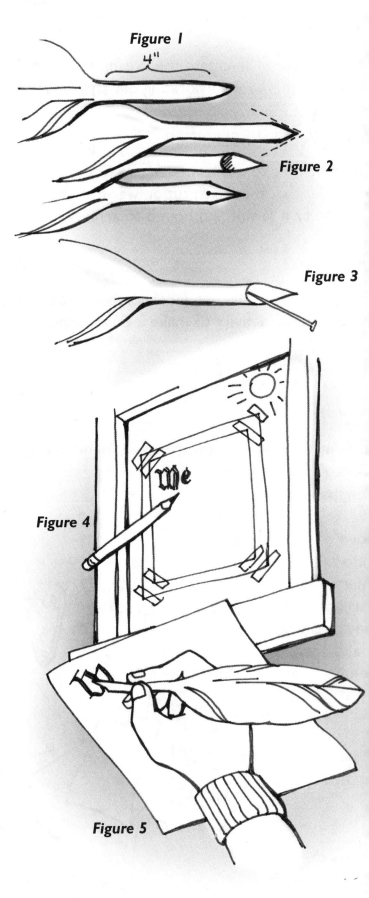

Figure 1

Figure 2

Figure 3

Figure 4

Figure 5

Sample Preamble

We the People of the United States,

in order to form a more perfect Union,
establish justice,
insure domestic tranquility,
provide for the common defense,
promote the general welfare,
and secure the blessings of liberty
to ourselves and our posterity,
do ordain and establish
this Constitution
for the United States of America

signed _____

Teacher Notes
Article I: Legislative Power

Objectives
☆ To understand the contents of the powers of the Legislative Branch of the American government
☆ To be able to explain the differences in powers between the Senate and the House of Representatives
☆ To be able to explain the qualifications of a senator and a member of the House of Representatives

Vocabulary

legislation	Laws
apportioned	Divided or distributed
enumeration	To count
executive	A person who is empowered to lead and manage
impeach	Bringing a public charge before a legal tribunal
adjourn	To close a meeting
compel	To force or to make someone to do something
treason	The betrayal of one's country
duties	Fees paid to the government to import or export goods
imports	Fees paid on goods being imported into a country
excises	Fees or taxes imposed on manufactured goods
naturalization	The process of becoming a citizen in a country not of one's birth
tribunals	Courts or seats where judgment occurs
letters of marque	Letter authorizing a government official to take action against an enemy or enemy citizens
writ of habeas corpus	An order stating when and why a person is being detained
bill of attainder	A piece of legislation passed by a legislature that declares a group or single person guilty of a crime and punishes them in some way without the benefit of a trial
ex poste facto law	To make something illegal after it has already happened
emolument	Pay for work performed

Background Information

The Constitution was written to secure a government that would last. However, many of the framers were skeptical of government and of human nature. They wanted to create a government that could balance the best and the worst of each.

In the *Federalist* Number 51, Madison wrote: "It may be a reflection on human nature, that such devices should be necessary to control the abuses of government. But what is government itself but the greatest of all reflections on human nature? If men were angels, no government would be necessary. If angels were to govern men, neither external or internal controls of government would be necessary. In framing government which is to be administered by men over men, the great difficulty lies in this: you must first enable the government to control the governed; and in the next place oblige it to control self. A dependence on the people is, no doubt, the primary control on the government; but experience has taught mankind the necessity of auxiliary precautions."

The Constitution is laid out in a Preamble and seven sections or Articles:

Article I: Legislative Power
Article II: Executive Power
Article III: Judicial Power
Article IV: States' Powers
Article V: Amending the Constitution
Article VI: Supremacy of Federal Power
Article VII: Ratification Process

In this book, the passages within the Constitution that are underlined were in the original document but have been amended by later Amendments to the Constitution that changed the original.

Suggested Lesson Plan

1. Explain the lesson objectives. Review the vocabulary and background information with the class.

2. Pass out page 36 to the class. Invite the students to read the handout and follow the directions. They should look up the words in the dictionary and explain their meaning in their own words.

3. It is important that the students know what is in each Article of the Constitution. They can do this by creating their own simple mnemonic device to help them.

Just as the word *HOMES* is a mnemonic device for remembering the names of the Great Lakes—Huron, Ontario, Michigan, Erie and Superior—students can create their own by taking the first letter from what each Article of the Constitution addresses and writing a sentence.

Share this old favorite mnemonic device for remembering the order of the planets with your students:

Mercury	My
Venus	Very
Earth	Educated
Mars	Mother
Jupiter	Just
Saturn	Served
Uranus	Us
Neptune	Nine
Pluto	Pickles

Share the following descriptions of the seven Articles with your students and what each Article of the Constitution deals with. Share the mnemonic device, Loud Elves Jingle Sleigh bells And Shout Raucously, with your students. Then invite them to write their own sentence that will help them remember what is in each Article of the Constitution.

Article I:	**L**egislative Power	Loud
Article II:	**E**xecutive Power	Elves
Article III:	**J**udicial Power	Jingle
Article IV:	**S**tates' Powers	Sleigh bells
Article V:	**A**mending the Constitution	And
Article VI:	**S**upremacy of Federal Power	Shout
Article VII:	**R**atification Process	Raucously

Remind students that the sentence they create will help them when they are answering questions about what each Article is about later.

4. Invite students to read Article 1 of the Constitution about the Legislative Branch of the American government. Then give them either or both of the handouts (pages 43-44) about the Senate and House of Representatives to complete.

Vocabulary Study

Look up each of the words below in the dictionary and write the definition in your own words. Words to look for as you study the Constitution:

legislation _____

apportioned _____

enumeration _____

executive _____

impeach _____

adjourn _____

compel _____

treason _____

duties _____

imports _____

excises _____

naturalization _____

tribunals _____

letters of marque _____

writ of habeas corpus _____

bill of attainder _____

ex poste facto law _____

emolument _____

Article I

Section 1. All legislative powers herein granted shall be vested in a Congress of the United States, which shall consist of a Senate and House of Representatives.

Section 2. The House of Representatives shall be composed of members chosen every second year by the people of the several states, and the electors in each state shall have the qualifications requisite for electors of the most numerous branch of the state legislature.

No person shall be a Representative who shall not have attained to the age of twenty-five years, and been seven years a citizen of the United States, and who shall not, when elected, be an inhabitant of that state in which he shall be chosen.

Representatives and direct taxes shall be apportioned among the several states which may be included within this Union, according to their respective numbers, which shall be determined by adding to the whole number of free persons, including those bound to service for a term of years, and excluding Indians not taxed, three-fifths of all other Persons. The actual Enumeration shall be made within three years after the first meeting of the Congress of the United States, and within every subsequent term of ten years, in such manner as they shall by law direct. The number of Representatives shall not exceed one for every thirty thousand, but each state shall have at least one Representative; and until such enumeration shall be made, the state of New Hampshire shall be entitled to choose three, Massachusetts eight, Rhode Island and Providence Plantations one, Connecticut five, New York six, New Jersey four, Pennsylvania eight, Delaware one, Maryland six, Virginia ten, North Carolina five, South Carolina five, and Georgia three.

When vacancies happen in the Representation from any state, the executive authority thereof shall issue writs of election to fill such vacancies.

The House of Representatives shall choose their speaker and other officers; and shall have the sole power of impeachment.

Section 3. The Senate of the United States shall be composed of two senators from each state, _chosen by the legislature thereof, for six years; and each senator shall have one vote._

Immediately after they shall be assembled in consequence of the first election, they shall be divided as equally as may be into three classes. The seats of the senators of the first class shall be vacated at the expiration of the second year, of the second class at the expiration of the fourth year, and the third class at the expiration of the sixth year, so that one-third may be chosen every second year; and if vacancies happen by resignation, or otherwise, during the recess of the legislature of any state, the executive thereof may make temporary appointments until the next meeting of the legislature, which shall then fill such vacancies.

No person shall be a senator who shall not have attained to the age of thirty years, and been nine years a citizen of the United States and who shall not, when elected, be an inhabitant of that state for which he shall be chosen.

The Vice President of the United States shall be President of the Senate, but shall have no vote, unless they be equally divided.

The Senate shall choose their other officers, and also a President pro tempore, in the absence of the Vice President, or when he shall exercise the office of President of the United States.

The Senate shall have the sole power to try all impeachments. When sitting for that purpose, they shall be on oath or affirmation. When the President of the United States is tried, the Chief Justice shall preside: And no person shall be convicted without the concurrence of two thirds of the members present.

Judgment in cases of impeachment shall not extend further than to removal from office, and disqualification to hold and enjoy any office of honor, trust or profit under the United States: but the party convicted shall nevertheless be liable and subject to indictment, trial, judgment and punishment, according to law.

Section 4. The times, places and manner of holding elections for senators and representatives, shall be prescribed in each state by the legislature thereof; but the Congress may at any time by law make or alter such regulations, except as to the places of choosing senators.

The Congress shall assemble at least once in every year, and such meeting shall be on the _first Monday in December,_ unless they shall by law appoint a different day.

...Senators and Representatives

Section 5. Each House shall be the judge of the elections, returns and qualifications of its own members, and a majority of each shall constitute a quorum to do business; but a smaller number may adjourn from day to day, and may be authorized to compel the attendance of absent members, in such manner, and under such penalties as each House may provide.

Each House may determine the rules of its proceedings, punish its members for disorderly behavior, and, with the concurrence of two-thirds, expel a member.

Each House shall keep a journal of its proceedings, and from time to time publish the same, excepting such parts as may in their judgment require secrecy; and the yeas and nays of the members of either House on any question shall, at the desire of one-fifth of those present, be entered on the journal.

Neither House, during the session of Congress, shall, without the consent of the other, adjourn for more than three days, nor to any other place than that in which the two Houses shall be sitting.

Section 6. The senators and representatives shall receive a compensation for their services, to be ascertained by law, and paid out of the treasury of the United States. They shall in all cases, except treason, felony and breach of the peace, be privileged from arrest during their attendance at the session of their respective Houses, and in going to and returning from the same; and for any speech or debate in either House, they shall not be questioned in any other place.

No senator or representative shall, during the time for which he was elected, be appointed to any civil office under the authority of the United States, which shall have been created, or the emoluments whereof shall have been increased during such time: and no person holding any office under the United States, shall be a member of either House during his continuance in office.

Section 7. All bills for raising revenue shall originate in the House of Representatives; but the Senate may propose or concur with amendments as on other bills.

Every bill which shall have passed the House of Representatives and the Senate, shall, before it become a law, be presented to the President of the United States; if he approve he shall sign it, but if not he shall return it, with his objections to that House in which it shall have originated, who shall enter the objections at large on their journal, and proceed to reconsider it. If after such reconsideration two-thirds of that House shall agree to pass the bill, it shall be sent, together with the objections, to the other House, by which it shall likewise be reconsidered, and if approved by two-thirds of that House, it shall become a law. But in all such cases the votes of both Houses shall be determined by yeas and nays, and the names of the persons voting for and against the bill shall be entered on the journal of each House respectively. If any bill shall not be returned by the President within ten days (Sundays excepted) after it shall have been presented to him, the same shall be a law, in like manner as if he had signed it, unless the Congress by their adjournment prevent its return, in which case it shall not be a law.

Every order, resolution, or vote to which the concurrence of the Senate and House of Representatives may be necessary (except on a question of adjournment) shall be presented to the President of the United States; and before the same shall take effect, shall be approved by him, or being disapproved by him, shall be repassed by two-thirds of the Senate and House of Representatives, according to the rules and limitations prescribed in the case of a bill.

Section 8. The Congress shall have power to lay and collect taxes, duties, imports and excises, to pay the debts and provide for the common defense and general welfare of the United States; but all duties, imports and excises shall be uniform throughout the United States;

To borrow money on the credit of the United States;

To regulate commerce with foreign nations, and among the several states, and with the Indian tribes;

To establish a uniform rule of naturalization, and uniform laws on the subject of bankruptcies throughout the United States;

To coin money, regulate the value thereof, and of foreign coin, and fix the standard of weights and measures;

To provide for the punishment of counterfeiting the securities and current coin of the United States;

To establish post offices and post roads;

To promote the progress of science and useful arts, by securing for limited times to authors and inventors the exclusive right to their respective writings and discoveries;

To constitute tribunals inferior to the Supreme Court;

To define and punish piracies and felonies committed on the high seas, and offenses against the law of nations;

To declare war, grant letters of marque and reprisal, and make rules concerning captures on land and water;

To raise and support armies, but no appropriation of money to that use shall be for a longer term than two years;

To provide and maintain a navy;

To make rules for the government and regulation of the land and naval forces;

To provide for calling forth the militia to execute the laws of the Union, suppress insurrections and repel invasions;

To provide for organizing, arming, and disciplining, the militia, and for governing such part of them as may be employed in the service of the United States, reserving to the states respectively, the appointment of the officers, and the authority of training the militia according to the discipline prescribed by Congress;

To exercise exclusive legislation in all cases whatsoever, over such district (not exceeding ten miles square) as may, by cession of particular states, and the acceptance of Congress, become the seat of the government of the United States, and to exercise like authority over all places purchased by the consent of the legislature of the state in which the same shall be, for the erection of forts, magazines, arsenals, dockyards, and other needful buildings;—And

To make all laws which shall be necessary and proper for carrying into execution the foregoing powers, and all other powers vested by this Constitution in the government of the United States, or in any department or officer thereof.

U.S. Mint

Army and Navy Militia

U.S. Post Office...

Section 9. The migration or importation of such persons as any of the states now existing shall think proper to admit, shall not be prohibited by the Congress prior to the year one thousand eight hundred and eight, but a tax or duty may be imposed on such importation, not exceeding ten dollars for each person.

The privilege of the writ of habeas corpus shall not be suspended, unless when in cases of rebellion or invasion the public safety may require it.

No bill of attainder or ex post facto law shall be passed.

No capitation, or other direct, tax shall be laid, unless in proportion to the census or enumeration herein before directed to be taken.

No tax or duty shall be laid on articles exported from any state.

No preference shall be given by any regulation of commerce or revenue to the ports of one state over those of another: nor shall vessels bound to, or from, one state, be obliged to enter, clear or pay duties in another.

No money shall be drawn from the treasury, but in consequence of appropriations made by law; and a regular statement and account of receipts and expenditures of all public money shall be published from time to time.

No title of nobility shall be granted by the United States: and no person holding any office of profit or trust under them, shall, without the consent of the Congress, accept of any present, emolument, office, or title, of any kind whatever, from any king, prince, or foreign state.

Section 10. No state shall enter into any treaty, alliance, or confederation; grant letters of marque and reprisal; coin money; emit bills of credit; make anything but gold and silver coin a tender in payment of debts; pass any bill of attainder, ex post facto law, or law impairing the obligation of contracts, or grant any title of nobility.

No state shall, without the consent of the Congress, lay any imports or duties on imports or exports, except what may be absolutely necessary for executing its inspection laws: and the net produce of all duties and imports, laid by any state on imports or exports, shall be for the use of the treasury of the United States; and all such laws shall be subject to the revision and control of the Congress.

No state shall, without the consent of Congress, lay any duty of tonnage, keep troops, or ships of war in time of peace, enter into any agreement or compact with another state, or with a foreign power, or engage in war, unless actually invaded, or in such imminent danger as will not admit of delay.

Senators and Representatives

1. List the qualifications to be a member of the House of Representatives.

_____

_____

_____

2. How are the numbers of the representatives in the House of Representatives determined?

_____

3. Who appoints a person to fill a House of Representative's seat if a representative dies in office?

_____

4. How long is the term for a member of the House of Representatives?

_____

5. List the qualifications to be a senator.

_____

_____

_____

6. Who serves as president of the Senate?

_____

7. How many senators serve in the Senate from each state?

_____

Name _____

The Senate and the House

A. Members of this body must be at least 30 years old to serve.
B. Draws up articles of impeachment.
C. Tries cases of impeachment.
D. Revenue-raising bills start in this body of the legislature.
E. Members of this body serve two-year terms.
F. Members of this body serve six-year terms.
G. Members of this body must be at least 25 years old to serve.
H. Vice President votes in this body in cases of a tie vote.

House

1.
2.
3.
4.
5.
6.
7.
8.

Senate

1. _____
2. _____
3. _____
4. _____
5. _____
6. _____
7. _____
8. _____

☆☆☆ Government Tree ☆☆☆

Objective

☆ To understand the various levels of government that are interconnected yet separate as defined by the Constitution.

Background Information

A tree, large and small branches, leaves, etc., all visually represent the branches of government and their division. They are interconnecting and yet separate as the Constitution states.

For individual or group projects

Materials

X-acto™ knife

1/4 cup of plaster of Paris

water

Styrofoam™ cup

mixing bowl

(trunk) balsa wood—1/2" x 1/2" x 17" long

(branches) balsa wood—3/8" x 3/16" x 36" long

(twigs) 1/8" x 1/8" x 36"

white glue

3" x 5" index cards—three colors

clear tape

black felt tip pen

scissors

Directions

1. Review the contents of this chapter and discuss the various branches of government. Explain the levels of government. Ask: How are the branches of the government interconnected? How are they separate and why? Direct students to go online to further research the specific divisions of each governmental branch.

2. Prepare one colored 3" x 5" index card. Use the same color code for the individual departments and divisions of each branch. Cut the color-coded cards into thirds and write down the departments and divisions. Follow the same process above for each government division and set aside.

3. Cut the "branches" of your tree ($^3/_8$" x $^3/_{16}$" x 36" long balsa wood) into 6" long strips. Make two slits on each side of the "trunk" ($^1/_2$" x $^1/_2$" x 17" long balsa wood) so that the "branches" will fit snugly inside. Make sure to balance out the "branches" around the "trunk." (Figure 1)

4. Cut various "twigs" ($^1/_8$" x $^1/_8$" x 36") in sizes ranging from 1" to 3". Carve small holes around the "branches" so that the "twigs" fit snugly inside. These twigs represent various divisions within a branch of government. Glue the "twigs" into the "branches" and set aside. (Figure 2).

5. Glue the "branches" of your governmental tree into the balsa wood "trunk" ($^1/_2$" x $^1/_2$" x 17" long) and set aside to dry. (Figure 3)

6. Follow the directions on the plaster of Paris and mix in the Styrofoam™ cup. Quickly slip the "trunk" into the mixture before it cures. Keep the tree steady from movement until it dries. (Figure 4)

7. Peel the Styrofoam™ cup off the plaster. Tape the color-coded government divisions onto the tree branches. Do this by taking the main branch title, i.e., *Justice* and affixing it to a top branch. Directly under that and in various places, the smaller divisions of the same branch should be affixed to the twigs and branches. Follow this process for the two remaining divisions until you have a governmental tree, which fully represents the United States government. (Figure 5)

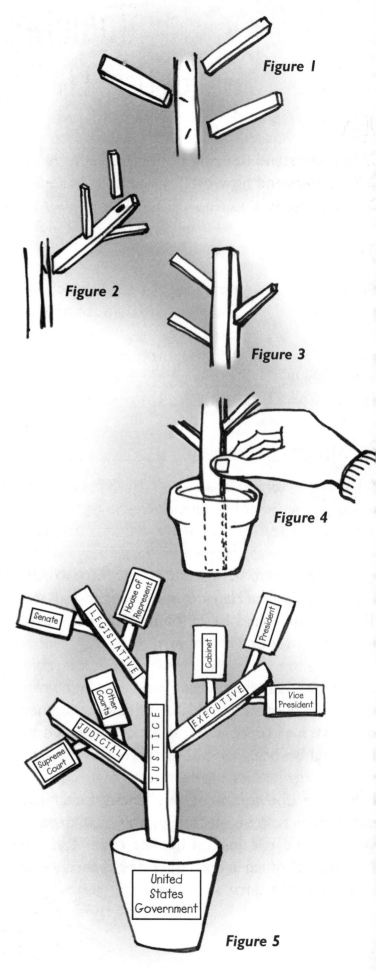

Figure 1

Figure 2

Figure 3

Figure 4

Figure 5

Teacher Notes
Article II: Executive Power

Objectives

☆ To understand the role of the President under the Constitution
☆ To understand how the President is elected
☆ To be able to describe the President's duties as laid out in the Constitution

Vocabulary

electors	Members of a special group designated to vote
quorum	The minimum number of people who need to be present for a vote of business to take place
oath	A formal promise
reprieves	Delays or postponements of punishment
pardon	To forgive a person of a crime or punishment

Background Information

When the Virginia Plan, a series of 15 resolutions proposed by Edmund Randolph, was introduced at the Constitutional Convention, the President was originally proposed to be a position elected by the legislature, not by the people. The executive, in the Virginia Plan would be elected to a single term and could be composed of more than one person serving in the role.

Later, in the New Jersey Plan, a series of nine resolutions proposed by William Paterson, the chief executive was to be a plural position elected by the legislative body and subject to removal by the presiding executives of the various states. Later during the convention, it was decided that the executive would be elected by the legislature, it would be a single person holding the office, and the term of office would be a single seven-year non-renewable term.

Eventually, the executive position evolved during the convention to what was ratified. However, one of the main difficulties for the delegates was to define how the President would be elected. From the very beginning, the President was not going to be elected by popular vote. At first it was thought that the legislative body would elect the President. But much debate centered around that proposal. There was fear from the small states that the large states would have too much control of the presidency if the vote was based on the size of the congressional delegation. At last, the electoral system that we have today was proposed and debated and changed and accepted.

Suggested Lesson Plan

1. Share the lesson objectives and the vocabulary with the students.
2. Distribute the "Article II" handout on pages 49-50. Invite students to read it, bearing in mind the vocabulary that was reinforced.
3. Distribute the handout on page 51 to students and invite them to answer the questions for review.
4. Distribute the handouts on pages 52-53. The first part details the vote tally for each candidate in each state for the 2000 election. The students are to tally the popular vote for each candidate in total. Also have them tally the popular vote by state. Invite them to color on the electoral map each state won by Albert Gore, Jr., in blue, each state won by George Walker Bush in red. Then ask them to tally the electoral votes won by each candidate.

Ask the students the following questions:
Who won the popular vote?
Who won the electoral count?
Who became President in 2000?

As a follow-up activity, ask the students to research presidential elections to identify the other candidates in American history who became President by winning the electoral vote but not the popular vote.

The following text is the original language from the Constitution. The passages that are underlined were later changed by the Amendment process.

48

Article II

Section 1. The executive power shall be vested in a President of the United States of America. He shall hold his office during the term of four years, and, together with the Vice President, chosen for the same term, be elected, as follows:

Each state shall appoint, in such manner as the Legislature thereof may direct, a number of electors, equal to the whole number of senators and representatives to which the State may be entitled in the Congress: but no senator or representative, or person holding an office of trust or profit under the United States, shall be appointed an elector.

The electors shall meet in their respective states, and vote by ballot for two persons, of whom one at least shall not be an inhabitant of the same state with themselves. And they shall make a list of all the persons voted for, and of the number of votes for each; which list they shall sign and certify, and transmit sealed to the seat of the government of the United States, directed to the president of the Senate. The president of the Senate shall, in the presence of the Senate and House of Representatives, open all the certificates, and the votes shall then be counted. The person having the greatest number of votes shall be the President, if such number be a majority of the whole number of electors appointed; and if there be more than one who have such majority, and have an equal number of votes, then the House of Representatives shall immediately choose by ballot one of them for President; and if no person have a majority, then from the five highest on the list the said House shall in like manner choose the President. But in choosing the President, the votes shall be taken by states, the representation from each state having one vote; A quorum for this purpose shall consist of a member or members from two-thirds of the states, and a majority of all the states shall be necessary to a choice. In every case, after the choice of the President, the person having the greatest number of votes of the electors shall be the Vice President. But if there should remain two or more who have equal votes, the Senate shall choose from them by ballot the Vice President.

The Congress may determine the time of choosing the electors, and the day on which they shall give their votes; which day shall be the same throughout the United States.

No person except a natural born citizen, or a citizen of the United States at the time of the adoption of this Constitution, shall be eligible to the office of President; neither shall any person be eligible to that office who shall not have attained to the age of thirty-five years, and been fourteen years a resident within the United States.

In case of the removal of the President from office, or of his death, resignation, or inability to discharge the powers and duties of the said office, the same shall devolve on the Vice President, and the Congress may by law provide for the case of removal, death, resignation or inability, both of the President and Vice President, declaring what officer shall then act as President, and such officer shall act accordingly, until the disability be removed, or a President shall be elected.

The President shall, at stated times, receive for his services, a compensation, which shall neither be increased nor diminished during the period for which he shall have been elected, and he shall not receive within that period any other emolument from the United States, or any of them.

Before he enter on the execution of his office, he shall take the following oath or affirmation:— "I do solemnly swear (or affirm) that I will faithfully execute the office of President of the United States, and will to the best of my ability, preserve, protect and defend the Constitution of the United States."

Section 2. The President shall be commander in chief of the Army and Navy of the United States, and of the militia of the several states, when called into the actual service of the United States; he may require the opinion, in writing, of the principal officer in each of the executive departments, upon any subject relating to the duties of their respective offices, and he shall have power to grant reprieves and pardons for offenses against the United States, except in cases of impeachment.

He shall have power, by and with the advice and consent of the Senate, to make treaties, provided two-thirds of the senators present concur; and he shall nominate, and by and with the advice and consent of the Senate, shall appoint ambassadors, other public ministers and consuls, judges of the Supreme Court, and all other officers of the United States, whose appointments are not herein otherwise provided for, and which shall be established by law: but the Congress may by law vest the appointment of such inferior officers, as they think proper, in the President alone, in the courts of law, or in the heads of departments.

The President shall have power to fill up all vacancies that may happen during the recess of the Senate, by granting commissions which shall expire at the end of their next session.

Section 3. He shall from time to time give to the Congress information of the state of the Union, and recommend to their consideration such measures as he shall judge necessary and expedient; he may, on extraordinary occasions, convene both Houses, or either of them, and in case of disagreement between them, with respect to the time of adjournment, he may adjourn them to such time as he shall think proper; he shall receive ambassadors and other public ministers; he shall take care that the laws be faithfully executed, and shall commission all the officers of the United States.

Section 4. The President, Vice President and all civil officers of the United States, shall be removed from office on impeachment for, and conviction of, treason, bribery, or other high crimes and misdemeanors.

The President
of the United States

Name _____

The President

1. List three qualifications to be President of the United States.

_____

_____

_____

2. Which branch of government is the President a part of—the executive, legislative or judicial?

_____

3. Who becomes President if the President dies in office?

_____

4. How long is the term of office for President?

_____

5. Write the oath of office the President says upon taking office.

_____

_____

_____

6. List three duties of the President.

_____

_____

_____

2000 Presidential Election

State	Total	George Bush	Al Gore	Ralph Nader	Patrick Buchanan	Other
AL	1,666,272	941,173	692,611	18,323	6,351	7,814
AK	285,560	167,398	79,004	28,747	5,192	5,219
AR	921,781	472,940	422,768	13,421	7,358	5,294
AZ	1,532016	781,652	685,341	45,645	12,373	7,005
CA	10,965,856	4,567,429	5,861,203	418,707	44,987	75,530
CO	1,741,368	883,748	738,227	91,434	10,465	17,494
CT	1,459,525	561,094	816,015	64,452	4,731	13,233
DE	327,622	137,288	180,068	8,307	777	1,182
FL	5,963,110	2,912,790	2,912,253	97,488	17,484	23,095
GA	2,596,645	1,419,720	1,116,230	13,273	10,926	36,496
HI	367,951	137,845	205,286	21,623	1,071	2,126
ID	501,621	336,937	138,637	12,292	7,615	6,140
IL	4,742,123	2,019,421	2,589,026	103,759	16,106	13,811
IN	2,199,302	1,245,836	901,980	18,531	16,959	15,996
IA	1,315,563	634,373	638,517	29,374	5,731	7,568
KS	1,072,218	622,332	399,276	36,086	7,370	7,154
KY	1,544,187	872,492	638,898	23,192	4,173	5,432
LA	1,765,656	927,871	792,344	20,473	14,356	10,612
ME	651,817	286,616	319,951	37,127	4,443	3,680
MD	2,020,480	813,797	1,140,782	53,768	4,248	7,885
MA	2,702,984	878,502	1,616,487	173,564	11,149	23,282
MI	4,232,711	1,953,139	2,170,418	84,165	2,061	22,928
MN	2,438,685	1,109,659	1,168,266	126,696	22,166	11,898
MS	994,184	572,844	404,614	8,122	2,265	6,339
MO	2,359,892	1,189,924	1,111,138	38,515	9,818	10,497
MT	410,997	240,178	137,126	24,437	5,697	3,559
NE	697,019	433,862	231,780	24,540	3,646	3,191
NV	608,970	301,575	279,978	15,008	4,747	7,662
NH	569,081	273,559	266,348	22,198	2,615	4,361
NJ	3,187,226	1,284,173	1,788,850	94,554	6,989	12,660
NM	598,605	286,417	286,783	21,251	1,392	2,762
NY	6,821,999	2,403,374	4,107,697	244,030	31,599	35,299
NC	2,911,262	1,631,163	1,257,692		8,874	13,533
ND	288,256	174,852	95,284	9,486	7,288	1,346
OH	4,701,998	2,350,363	2,183,628	117,799	26,721	23,484
OK	1,234,229	744,337	474,276		9,014	6,602
OR	1,533,968	713,577	720,342	77,357	7,063	15,629
PA	4,913,119	2,281,127	2,485,967	103,392	16,023	26,610
RI	409,047	130,555	249,508	25,052	2,273	1,659
SC	1,382,717	785,937	565,561	20,200	3,519	7,500
SD	316,269	190,700	118,804		3,322	3,443
TN	2,076,181	1,061,949	981,720	19,781	4,250	8,481
TX	6,407,637	3,799,639	2,433,746	137,994	12,394	23,864
UT	770,754	515,096	203,053	35,850	9,319	7,436
VT	294,308	119,775	149,022	20,374	2,192	2,945
VA	2,739,447	1,437,490	1,217,290	59,398	5,455	19,814
WA	2,487,433	1,108,864	1,247,652	103,002	7,171	20,744
WV	648,124	336,475	295,497	10,680	3,169	2,303
WI	2,598,607	1,237,279	1,242,987	94,070	11,446	12,825
WY	218,351	147,947	60,481	4,625	2,724	,574
DC	201,894	18,073	171,923	10,576		1,322

TLC10541 Copyright © Teaching & Learning Company, Carthage, IL 62321-0010

Name _____

2000 Presidential Electoral Map

Washington–11
Montana–3
North Dakota–3
Minnesota–10
New Hampshire–4
Maine–4
Vermont–3
Oregon–7
Idaho–4
South Dakota–3
Wisconsin–11
Massachusetts–12
Wyoming–3
Michigan–18
New York–33
Rhode Island–4
Connecticut–8
Nevada–4
Iowa–7
Pennsylvania–23
New Jersey–15
Utah–5
Nebraska–5
Indiana–12
Ohio–21
Delaware–3
Illinois–22
West Virginia–5
Maryland–10
California–54
Colorado–8
Kansas–6
Missouri–11
Kentucky–8
Virginia–13
Washington, D.C.–3
North Carolina–14
Arizona–8
New Mexico–5
Oklahoma–8
Arkansas–6
Tennessee–11
South Carolina–8
Mississippi–7
Alabama–9
Georgia–13
Texas–32
Louisiana–9
Florida–25

Hawaii–4
Alaska–3

Electoral Votes

Using the information found on the map and page 52,
calculate how many electoral votes each nominee received in the 2000 election.
The District of Columbia has three votes.
There was an abstention in the 2000 election.

Bush _____   Gore _____

Nader _____   Buchanan _____

Other _____

☆☆☆ Presidents Board Game ☆☆☆

Objective

☆ This board game will help students become familiar with the United States Presidents, the year of their presidencies and the states in which they were born.

Background Information

The President of the United States of America is the head of state and the executive branch of the federal government. It is his or her role to enforce laws in the Constitution.

*Prior knowledge required
*Two to six players

Materials

laminated wall map of the United States
scissors
poster board
ruler or T-square

laminator/clear, self-adhesive paper
President Cards (pages 57-60)
double-sided tape

Directions

1. Players should review this chapter of the Constitution. Discuss the qualifications of a President. Players should write a series of questions and answers to equal the amount of Presidents. For example, if there are 44 Presidents and four players, then each player must write 11 questions. The questions should be varied, such as: How old must a person be to become the United States President? How many terms is a President allowed to serve in office? What is a term? Ask players to review the question lists with each other to make sure there are no repeats. Set lists aside for later.

2. Have players study the "Presidents' Birthplace Chart" on page 56. Cut out the President Cards and laminate.

3. Set up the laminated wall map. Mount the back of the President Cards with double-sided tape and position them in order at the bottom of the map. Follow the chart for guidance.

4. Establish a moderator for the game who will read the questions, give points for correct answers and insure that the President Cards are placed in the proper locations on the map. The moderator will give a second point to the player if the birthplace for each President is properly located.

TLC10541 Copyright © Teaching & Learning Company, Carthage, IL 62321-0010

How to Play the Game

. The moderator asks the first player a question that was prepared earlier by the moderator. If the player answers the question correctly, he or she receives one point. The player will go to the wall map and pull the first President Card from the lineup and place it on the correct presidential birthplace. The moderator verifies the President's birthplace from the chart (page 56). If the player is correct, then another point is given.

. If the player chooses the wrong presidential birthplace, no point is given. The President Card is placed back in the lineup. Play continues with the second player answering a question properly, choosing the next President Card and placing it on the correct birth location on the map.

. Game ends when all the Presidents have been placed on or near their birth location. If questions run out during the course of play, they may be repeated. The player with the most points wins.

Presidents' Birthplace Chart

Years in Office	Sequence	Presidential Name	State of Birth
1789-1797	1st	George Washington	VA
1797-1801	2nd	John Adams	MA
1801-1809	3rd	Thomas Jefferson	VA
1809-1817	4th	James Madison	VA
1817-1825	5th	James Monroe	VA
1825-1829	6th	John Quincy Adams	MA
1829-1837	7th	Andrew Jackson	SC
1837-1841	8th	Martin Van Buren	NY
1841-1841	9th	William Henry Harrison	VA
1841-1845	10th	John Tyler	VA
1845-1849	11th	James K. Polk	NC
1849-1850	12th	Zachary Taylor	VA
1850-1853	13th	Millard Fillmore	NY
1853-1857	14th	Franklin Pierce	NH
1857-1861	15th	James Buchanan	PA
1861-1865	16th	Abraham Lincoln	KY
1865-1869	17th	Andrew Johnson	NC
1869-1877	18th	Ulysses S. Grant	OH
1877-1881	19th	Rutherford B. Hayes	OH
1881-1881	20th	James A. Garfield	OH
1881-1885	21st	Chester A. Arthur	VT
1885-1889	22nd	Grover Cleveland	NJ
1889-1893	23rd	Benjamin Harrison	OH
1893-1897	24th	Grover Cleveland	NJ
1897-1901	25th	William McKinley	OH
1901-1909	26th	Theodore Roosevelt	NY
1909-1913	27th	William Howard Taft	OH
1913-1921	28th	Woodrow Wilson	VA
1921-1923	29th	Warren G. Harding	OH
1923-1929	30th	Calvin Coolidge	VT
1929-1933	31st	Herbert Hoover	IA
1933-1945	32nd	Franklin D. Roosevelt	NY
1945-1953	33rd	Harry S. Truman	MO
1953-1961	34th	Dwight D. Eisenhower	TX
1961-1963	35th	John F. Kennedy	MA
1963-1969	36th	Lyndon B. Johnson	TX
1969-1974	37th	Richard M. Nixon	CA
1974-1977	38th	Gerald R. Ford	NE
1977-1981	39th	Jimmy Carter	GA
1981-1989	40th	Ronald Reagan	IL
1989-1993	41st	George H. W. Bush	MA
1993-2001	42nd	William J. Clinton	AR
2001-2009	43rd	George W. Bush	CT

TLC10541 Copyright © Teaching & Learning Company, Carthage, IL 62321-001

Presidents Board Game Cards

Cut out each President stamp and laminate.

 1st George Washington	 2nd John Adams	 3rd Thomas Jefferson	 4th James Madison	 5th James Monroe
 11th James K. Polk	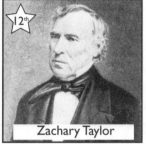 12th Zachary Taylor	 13th Millard Fillmore	 14th Franklin Pierce	 15th James Buchanan
 21st Chester A. Arthur	 22nd Grover Cleveland	 23rd Benjamin Harrison	 24th Grover Cleveland	 25th William McKinley
 31st Herbert Hoover	 32nd Franklin D. Roosevelt	 33rd Harry S. Truman	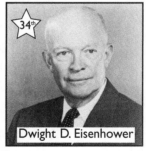 34th Dwight D. Eisenhower	 35th John F. Kennedy
 41st George H. W. Bush	 42nd William J. Clinton	 43rd George W. Bush	44th	45th

58

Presidents Board Game Cards

6th — John Quincy Adams

7th — Andrew Jackson

8th — Martin Van Buren

9th — William Henry Harrison

10th — John Tyler

16th — Abraham Lincoln

17th — Andrew Johnson

18th — Ulysses S. Grant

19th — Rutherford B. Hayes

20th — James A. Garfield

26th — Theodore Roosevelt

27th — William Howard Taft

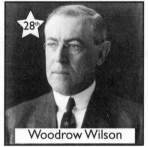
28th — Woodrow Wilson

29th — Warren G. Harding

30th — Calvin Coolidge

36th — Lyndon B. Johnson

37th — Richard M. Nixon

38th — Gerald R. Ford

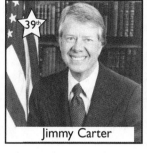
39th — Jimmy Carter

40th — Ronald Reagan

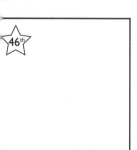
46th

47th

48th

49th

50th

60

Teacher Notes
Articles III Through VII

Objectives
☞ To understand and be able to describe the three branches of government and their duties
☞ To understand the process for admitting new states
☞ To understand the ways that the Constitution can be amended

Vocabulary

treason	Levying war against the United States or giving aid and comfort to the enemy
maritime	Having to do with sea and navigation
original jurisdiction	The court that has the right to hear a case for the first time
appellate jurisdiction	The court that hears a case on appeal or the second time a case is heard

Background Information

Article III

Article III establishes the judicial branch of government, which is the last of the co-equal three parts of the United States government. Section I also gives the Congress the jurisdiction to establish lower courts. Section 2 of Article III establishes where court cases should be heard first. And Section 3 defines *treason* and the punishment for

Article IV

Article IV details how states are to work with each other including honoring the official acts of the other states. The Article also provides for the return of criminals and runaway slaves. The clause to return runaway slaves became null and void when slavery was outlawed in a latter amendment.

Article Five

Article V describes the ways in which the Constitution can be amended.

Article VI

Article VI has three sections. Section I states that the United States will assume the debts incurred before the Constitution went into effect. Section 2 says that federal law and treaties are the law of the land. Section 3 requires that government officials must take an oath of office and that religion or religious beliefs cannot be a barrier to service.

Article VII

Article VII describes the method by which the Constitution would be ratified.

Suggested Lesson Plan

1. Explain the lesson objectives.
2. Review the vocabulary and background information with the class.
3. Invite students to read the "Articles III Through VII" handout on pages 67-68 on their own.
4. Invite students to answer the questions in the handout pertaining to Articles III through VII.

Article III

Section 1. The judicial power of the United States, shall be vested in one Supreme Court, and in such inferior courts as the Congress may from time to time ordain and establish. The judges, both of the supreme and inferior courts, shall hold their offices during good behavior, and shall, at stated times, receive for their services, a compensation, which shall not be diminished during their continuance in office.

Section 2. The judicial power shall extend to all cases, in law and equity, arising under this Constitution, the laws of the United States, and treaties made, or which shall be made, under their authority;—to all cases affecting ambassadors, other public ministers and consuls;—to all cases of admiralty and maritime jurisdiction;—to controversies to which the United States shall be a party;—to controversies between two or more states;—*between a state and citizens of another state;*—between citizens of different states;—between citizens of the same state claiming lands under grants of different states, and between a state, or the citizens thereof, and foreign states, citizens or subjects.

In all cases affecting ambassadors, other public ministers and consuls, and those in which a state shall be party, the Supreme Court shall have original jurisdiction. In all the other cases before mentioned, the Supreme Court shall have appellate jurisdiction, both as to law and fact, with such exceptions, and under such regulations as the Congress shall make.

The trial of all crimes, except in cases of impeachment, shall be by jury; and such trial shall be held in the state where the said crimes shall have been committed; but when not committed within any state, the trial shall be at such place or places as the Congress may by law have directed.

Section 3. Treason against the United States, shall consist only in levying war against them, or in adhering to their enemies, giving them aid and comfort. No person shall be convicted of treason unless on the testimony of two witnesses to the same overt act, or on confession in open court.

The Congress shall have power to declare the punishment of treason, but no attainder of treason shall work corruption of blood, or forfeiture except during the life of the person attained.

The Supreme Court

Article IV

Section 1. Full faith and credit shall be given in each state to the public acts, records, and judicial proceedings of every other state. And the Congress may by general laws prescribe the manner in which such acts, records, and proceedings shall be proved, and the effect thereof.

Section 2. The citizens of each state shall be entitled to all privileges and immunities of citizens in the several states.

A person charged in any state with treason, felony, or other crime, who shall flee from justice, and be found in another state, shall on demand of the executive authority of the state from which he fled, be delivered up, to be removed to the state having jurisdiction of the crime.

No person held to service or labor in one state, under the laws thereof, escaping into another, shall, in consequence of any law or regulation therein, be discharged from such service or labor, but shall be delivered up on claim of the party to whom such service or labor may be due.

Section 3. New states may be admitted by the Congress into this Union; but no new states shall be formed or erected within the jurisdiction of any other state; nor any state be formed by the junction of two or more states, or parts of states, without the consent of the legislatures of the states concerned as well as of the Congress.

The Congress shall have power to dispose of and make all needful rules and regulations respecting the territory or other property belonging to the United States; and nothing in this Constitution shall be so construed as to prejudice any claims of the United States, or of any particular state.

Section 4. The United States shall guarantee to every state in this Union a republican form of government, and shall protect each of them against invasion; and on application of the legislature, or of the executive (when the legislature cannot be convened) against domestic violence.

Concerning the States...

Article V

The Congress, whenever two-thirds of both houses shall deem it necessary, shall propose amendments to this Constitution, or, on the application of the legislatures of two-thirds of the several states, shall call a convention for proposing amendments, which, in either case, shall be valid to all intents and purposes, as part of this Constitution, when ratified by the legislatures of three-fourths of the several states, or by conventions in three-fourths thereof, as the one or the other mode of ratification may be proposed by the Congress; provided that no amendment which may be made prior to the year one thousand eight hundred and eight shall in any manner affect the first and fourth clauses in the ninth section of the first article; and that no state, without its consent, shall be deprived of its equal suffrage in the Senate.

Amending our Constitution...

AMENDMENT XXVI   **AMENDMENT XIII**   **AMENDMENT XIX**

Article VI

All debts contracted and engagements entered into, before the adoption of this Constitution, shall be as valid against the United States under this Constitution, as under the Confederation. This Constitution, and the laws of the United States which shall be made in pursuance thereof; and all treaties made, or which shall be made, under the authority of the United States, shall be the supreme law of the land; and the judges in every state shall be bound thereby, anything in the Constitution or laws of any State to the contrary notwithstanding.

The senators and representatives before mentioned, and the members of the several state legislatures, and all executive and judicial officers, both of the United States and of the several states, shall be bound by oath or affirmation, to support this Constitution; but no religious test shall ever be required as a qualification to any office or public trust under the United States.

65

Article VII

The ratification of the conventions of nine states, shall be sufficient for the establishment of this Constitution between the states so ratifying the same.

Done in convention by the unanimous consent of the states present the seventeenth day of September in the year of our Lord one thousand seven hundred and eighty-seven and of the independence of the United States of America the twelfth.

In witness whereof we have hereunto subscribed our names,

George Washington—President and deputy from Virginia

New Hampshire: John Langdon, Nicholas Gilman

Massachusetts: Nathaniel Gorham, Rufus King

Connecticut: William Samuel Johnson, Roger Sherman

New York: Alexander Hamilton

New Jersey: William Livingston, David Brearly, William Paterson, Jonathan Dayton

Pennsylvania: Benjamin Franklin, Thomas Mifflin, Robert Morris, George Clymer, Thomas FitzSimons, Jared Ingersoll, James Wilson, Gouverneur Morris

Delaware: George Read; Gunning Bedford, Jr.; John Dickinson; Richard Bassett; Jacob Broom

Maryland: James McHenry, Daniel of St. Thomas Jenifer, Daniel Carroll

Virginia: John Blair; James Madison, Jr.

North Carolina: William Blount, Richard Dobbs Spaight, Hugh Williamson

South Carolina: John Rutledge, Charles Cotesworth Pinckney, Charles Pinckney, Pierce Butler

Georgia: William Few, Abraham Baldwin

Name _____

Articles III Through VII

1. What branch of government is the Supreme Court in? _____

2. Explain *original jurisdiction.* _____

_____

3. In which cases does the Supreme Court have original jurisdiction? _____

_____

4. In the United States government, the framers were careful to set up checks and balances, so the various branches of government could check the power of the other branches. What

   check does the Supreme Court have on Congress? _____

_____

5. *Extradition* means that if a crime is committed in one area and the criminal escapes to another area, the place in which the criminal committed the crime can ask the place in which the criminal escaped to and was caught to return the criminal to the place of the crime to stand trial.

   Where is that concept guaranteed in the Constitution? _____

_____

6. The Constitution states that every state admitted will have what kind of government?

_____

7. Describe the two ways in which a constitutional amendment may be proposed.

1. _____

2. _____

8. What are the two modes of ratification of a constitutional amendment?

1. _____

2. _____

9. Who does Article VI state will pay for the debts incurred before the ratification of the

Constitution? _____

10. How many states had to ratify the Constitution before it became the law? _____

Bill of Rights Time Line

September 17, 1787

The Constitution was completed and signed in Philadelphia at the Pennsylvania State House and sent to the states for ratification. The framers had debated how amendments could be added to the new Constitution during the May to September convention. There had also been debate about adding a Bill of Rights even before the Constitution was finished.

George Mason of Virginia offered to write a bill of rights. He deeply distrusted powerful, centralized and autocratic government and believed that individual rights had to be protected. Though Mason had authored the Virginia Bill of Rights, the delegates voted down his proposal. Mason was so upset that the document did not include a bill of rights that he refused to sign the completed Constitution.

Article V of the Constitution, however, gave future generations a way to amend the document and assured that the debate and push for a bill of rights would continue.

1788

June 21, the ninth state, New Hampshire ratified the Constitution. The new Constitution went into effect. The new government began to take shape.

1789

April 1, the first House of Representatives was organized.

April 6, George Washington was elected President. He was greeted by cheering crowds from Virginia to New York. Washington was the most celebrated American of that time.

April 30, George Washington was inaugurated as the first President of the United States. He took the oath of office, required by the Constitution, on the balcony of the Federal Building in New York City.

June 8, James Madison, Congressman from Virginia, in the new House of Representatives offered amendments to the Constitution.

September 25, Congress submitted 12 amendments to the Constitution to the states for ratification. Only 10 were approved by the states at the state convention, these 10 became known as the Bill of Rights. The states held conventions to ratify the Bill of Rights. The following states ratified the Bill of Rights:

New Jersey	November 20, 1789
Maryland	December 19, 1789
North Carolina	December 22, 1789
New Hampshire	January 25, 1790
Delaware	January 28, 1790
New York	February 27, 1790
Pennsylvania	March 10, 1790
Rhode Island	June 7, 1790
Vermont*	November 3, 1791
Virginia	December 15, 1791

*On January 10, 1791, though not yet a state, Vermont ratified the Constitution. Vermont was admitted into the Union on March 4, 1791, as the fourteenth state.

Objectives

☆ Identify the five freedoms protected in the First Amendment
☆ Identify symbols found in the cartoons
☆ Identify elements of irony and satire
☆ Identify cartoonists' messages
☆ Identify historical symbols
☆ Explain what symbols mean
☆ Recognize the meaning and subject of each cartoon
☆ Judge messages found in the cartoons
☆ Compare and contrast viewpoints

Vocabulary

grievance   A situation thought unjust and reason for complaint and remedy

redress   To set right, often by making compensation for a wrong

Background Information

Some have argued eloquently that the First Amendment is the most important of the amendments in the Bill of Rights because of the importance of the five freedoms that are protected. The First Amendment protects five basic rights from the intrusion of our government—religion, speech, press, assembly and the redress of grievances.

Each cartoon in this section addresses one of the freedoms protected in the First Amendment.

First Amendment

The first part of the First Amendment protects the freedom of religion. The First Amendment protects religion in two ways; first, by keeping the government from establishing a state religion. This is called "The Establishment Clause." It simply means that the government cannot pass laws favoring one religion over another. In other words, Congress cannot make one religion the religion of the country, such as Catholicism was in France. Secondly, this amendment protects religion by allowing people to practice any religion they choose. This is referred to as "The Free Exercise Clause." Though Congress cannot pass laws curbing anyone's rights to believe anything they want, it can legislate to stop certain religious practices. For instance, Congress prohibits the practice of polygamy.

The first handout (page 77) relates to the First Amendment protection of freedom of religion and specifically "The Establishment Clause."

Not Allowed—Allowed

In this two-panel cartoon (page 78) drawn by Joe Heller, the central object in the first panel is a large stone monument with the Ten Commandments mounted on the front of the marker. The stone is placed in the town square in front of what looks like the courthouse. The second panel shows everything exactly the same, except placed next to the monument with the Ten Commandments is a sign that says, "HISTORICAL MARKER."

This cartoon was drawn after the 2005 Supreme Court ruled on two cases that had been brought before the Court regarding the display of the Ten Commandments. In the case brought before the Court from Texas, the Court upheld for the defendants who were displaying the Ten Commandments on Texas State Capitol grounds in Austin. Over 40 years ago the Fraternal Order of Eagles erected a six-foot monument with the Ten Commandments displayed on the front. Many such monuments were donated to public places across the country in honor of the Cecil B. DeMille movie, *The Ten Commandments*. The Court ruled that the display was historical, showing the Ten Commandments among other symbols. In a 5-4 decision, the Court ruled that it did not cross the line to the promotion of one religion over another.

The high Court ruled, however, against the defendants in Kentucky. County officials in McCreary County, Kentucky, had authorized the courts to display framed copies of the Ten Commandments. After complaints had been lodged against the county officials, legal advisors suggested that other legal documents mentioned God in them. This display was later changed to include documents that played a key role in the development of American law. The Court ruled against the officials in McCreary County because they said the officials had acted with improper intent. The purpose of the display, the Court believed, was to promote and advance one religion over another. Justice David Souter wrote, "When the government acts with the ostensible and predominant purpose of advancing religion, it violates the central Establishment Clause value of official religious neutrality."

TLC10541 Copyright © Teaching & Learning Company, Carthage, IL 62321-00

First Amendment

The second part of the First Amendment protects citizens' right to speak freely. Benjamin Franklin said, "Whoever would overthrow the liberty of a nation must begin by subduing the freeness of speech." The people who wrote the Bill of Rights believed this to be a most basic human right.

This right, though, has limitations. Speech can be limited if there is "a clear and present danger." In 1919, the Supreme Court case Schenck v. United States, the Supreme Court ruled that Schenck had distributed leaflets to men to encourage them to resist the draft. The government convicted Schenck under the Espionage Act. Schenck maintained that freedom of speech entitles him to be able to say whatever he wished. The Court ruled "We admit that in many places and in ordinary times the defendants, in saying all that was said in the circular, would have been within their constitutional rights. But the character of every act depends upon the circumstances in which it is done. . . The most stringent protection of free speech would not protect a man in falsely shouting fire in a theater, and causing a panic . . . The question in every case is whether the words used are in such circumstances and are of such a nature as to create a clear and present danger ... When a nation is at war, many things that might be said in time of peace are such a hindrance to its effort that their utterances will not be endured so long as men fight, and that no Court could regard them as protected by any constitutional right."

Protecting Democracy . . .

In this cartoon (page 80), a man is at a restaurant of some sort that has a number of television screens hanging from the ceiling. One is showing a man described as an armchair general. The next screen shows a pundit, and the next screen shows a shot of news coverage of a peace rally. A man is reading the newspaper in the corner of the frame. George W. Bush is sitting between the man talking and a man sitting next to him. The speaking bubble of the man says, "PROTECTING DEMOCRACY WOULD BE A LOT SIMPLER WITHOUT ALL THIS FREE SPEECH!"

First Amendment

The First Amendment also guarantees the freedom of the press. In a letter to Colonel Edward Carrington (January 16, 1787) Thomas Jefferson wrote, "Were it left to me to decide whether we should have a government without newspapers, or newspapers without a government, I should not hesitate a moment to prefer the latter." Jefferson and others knew and believed that a free and independent press was necessary in a democracy. The authors of the Virginia Bill of Rights recognized this when they wrote, "That the freedom of the press is one of the great bulwarks of liberty and can never be restrained but by a despotick government." But can the press print anything it wants to? No. There are restrictions on the freedom of speech. The same test of "clear and present danger" applies to the press.

The cartoon in this exercise (page 82), deals with a different concept concerning freedom of the press—keeping sources confidential.

Freedom of the Press...

The First Amendment (Amended)

In 1972, Peter Bridge, a reporter for the New Jersey newspaper, *Evening News*, who had reported on an Essex County, Newark housing scandal, was jailed when he refused to reveal his source for the story to a grand jury. It was reported that Peter Bridge answered more than 50 questions when he was in front of the grand jury, but he would not divulge his sources for the story. Bridge was the first reporter who was jailed after the Supreme Court case, Branzburg v. Hayes was handed down. In that case, the high court ruled that "the First Amendment does not relieve a newspaper reporter of the obligation that all citizens have to respond to a grand jury subpoena and answer questions relevant to a criminal investigation and therefore the Amendment does not afford him a constitutional testimonial privilege for an agreement he made to conceal facts relevant to a grand jury's investigation of a crime or to conceal the criminal conduct of his source or evidence thereof." (See cartoon on page 82.)

First Amendment

The right of the people to peaceably assemble gives people the right to gather and discuss, protest or march in favor of whatever subjects they choose. This right dates back to the revolutionary period in America and was specifically guaranteed by the Pennsylvania Declaration of Rights of 1776.

However, the court, in Cox v. Louisiana (1965), stated that it would not allow "demonstrations, however peaceful or commendable their motives, which conflict with properly drawn statutes and ordinances designed to promote law and order, protect the community against disorder, regulate traffic, safeguard legitimate interests in private and public property, or protect the administration of justice and other essential governmental functions." So, even though people have the right to protest and assemble in groups, to do so they still need to be mindful of regulations governing it. These include federal and state laws and local ordinances.

Dissent—As American as . . .

In this cartoon (page 84), Ann Telnaes, the cartoonist is comparing protesting to Mom and Apple Pie. Telnaes portrays a wholesome-looking, apron-clad motherly type complete with pot holder, holding a steaming hot apple pie in one hand as she holds a sign saying, "DISSENT" in the other.

First Amendment

The last of the five activities protected in the First Amendment is the right to "petition the government for a redress of grievances." This has long since been considered a right. It was protected under the English Bill of Rights in 1689. This simply means that a person has the right to circulate a piece of paper and gather names of people who agree with you that the government has done something wrong that you want fixed or changed.

Getting Signatures for the Petition

The very famous and Pulitzer Prize-winning cartoonist "Ding" Darling drew the cartoon on page 86 showing a man who started a petition for a new city government. In the first panel, it shows the man meekly asking his neighbor if he would sign the petition. The second panel shows the man surrounded by hundreds of enthusiastic signers to the petition as he calls out for more paper on which to sign. The third and last panel of the cartoon shows a petition several times longer than the man.

Freedom to Petition...

Suggested Lesson Plan

1. Share the vocabulary with your students.
2. Invite students to read the "Bill of Rights Time Line" handout on pages 69-70.
3. Share the text of the First Amendment with your students.
4. Ask your students to explain the First Amendment in their own words.
5. Use the editorial cartoon handouts to start class discussions about what each clause of the First Amendment means.

Amendment I

Congress shall make no law respecting an establishment of religion, or prohibiting the free exercise thereof; or abridging the freedom of speech, or of the press; or the right of the people peaceably to assemble, and to petition the government for a redress of grievances.

Name _____

Not Allowed–Allowed

By Joe Heller, Green Bay *Press-Gazette*

Study the editorial cartoon below.

© Joe Heller. Reprinted with permission.

Name _____

Not Allowed–Allowed

Cartoon by Joe Heller, Green Bay *Press-Gazette*

Amendment I

Congress shall make no law respecting an establishment of religion, or prohibiting the free exercise thereof; or abridging the freedom of speech, or of the press; or the right of the people peaceably to assemble, and to petition the government for a redress of grievances.

Study the editorial cartoon on page 78 and answer the following questions:

1. What religious symbol is shown in both panels of the cartoon?

_____

2. What about the drawing indicates what the religious symbol is?

_____

3. Who in the cartoon has announced the "Not Allowed—Allowed"?

_____

4. What sign is in the second panel that is not in the first panel?

_____

5. What does this religious symbol have to do with the Constitution?

_____

6. What guaranteed freedom is at stake in the cartoon?

_____

7. What message do you think the cartoonist is trying to convey?

_____

Name _____

Protecting Democracy...

By Joel Pett

Study the editorial cartoon below.

Joel Pett Editorial Cartoon © 2003 Joel Pett. Used with the permission of Joel Pett and the Cartoonist Group.

Protecting Democracy...

Cartoon by Joel Pett

Amendment I

Congress shall make no law respecting an establishment of religion, or prohibiting the free exercise thereof; or abridging the freedom of speech, or of the press; or the right of the people peaceably to assemble, and to petition the government for a redress of grievances.

Study the editorial cartoon on page 80 and answer the following questions:

1. Where does the cartoon take place?

   _____

2. Who is the political leader depicted in the cartoon?

   _____

3. What features indicate who the leader is?

   _____

4. Name the four different expressions of freedom of speech that are depicted in this cartoon, other than the man speaking?

   _____

5. Explain *irony* and how it relates to the man's statement in the cartoon.

   _____

Name _____

The First Amendment (Amended)

By Pat Oliphant

Study the editorial cartoon below.

Identify which one of the amendments
in the Bill of Rights this cartoon is concerned with.

_____

     TLC10541 Copyright © Teaching & Learning Company, Carthage, IL 62321-001

The First Amendment (Amended)

Cartoon by Pat Oliphant

Amendment I

Congress shall make no law respecting an establishment of religion, or prohibiting the free exercise thereof; or abridging the freedom of speech, or of the press; or the right of the people peaceably to assemble, and to petition the government for a redress of grievances.

Study the editorial cartoon on page 82 and answer the following questions:

1. Who does the man chained to the wall represent?

_____

2. What is he trying to do with his toes?

_____

3. Where is the man?

_____

4. What clues tell you where he is?

_____

5. How does a reporter revealing his or her sources for a story jeopardize freedom of the press?

_____

6. How is the cartoonist suggesting the First Amendment is being amended?

_____

7. If a reporter has to reveal his sources for a story, how could this limit freedom of the press?

_____

Name _____

Dissent–As American as...

By Ann Telnaes

Study the editorial cartoon below.

As American as

Identify which one of the amendments
in the Bill of Rights this cartoon is concerned with.

_____

Dissent–as American as...

Cartoon by Ann Telnaes

Amendment I

Congress shall make no law respecting an establishment of religion, or prohibiting the free exercise thereof; or abridging the freedom of speech, or of the press; or the right of the people peaceably to assemble, and to petition the government for a redress of grievances.

Study the editorial cartoon on page 84 and answer the following questions:

1. In this cartoon, the cartoonist, Ann Telnaes, depicts the woman holding two things—what are they?

_____

2. What does the sign DISSENT represent in the terms of First Amendment freedoms?

_____

3. In your opinion, how does the cartoonist view protesting?

_____

4. What two things does the cartoonist compare DISSENT to?

_____

5. In your opinion, why does the cartoonist compare *dissent* to these things?

_____

Name _____

Getting Signatures for the Petition

By "Ding" Darling (Jay Norwood Darling)

Study the editorial cartoon below.

"Getting Signatures for the Petition" first appeared in April 8, 1907. © J.N. "Ding" Darling.
Permission granted by the Special Collections at the University of Iowa Libraries.

Identify which one of the amendments in the Bill of Rights this cartoon is concerned with.

_____

Getting Signatures for the Petition

Cartoon by "Ding" Darling (Jay Norwood Darling)

Amendment I

Congress shall make no law respecting an establishment of religion, or prohibiting the free exercise thereof; or abridging the freedom of speech, or of the press; or the right of the people peaceably to assemble, and to petition the government for a redress of grievances.

Study the editorial cartoon on page 86 and answer the following questions:

1. What does the man talking in the first panel have in his hand?

   _____

2. What is he trying to get the others in the cartoon to do?

   _____

3. What happens in the second panel?

   _____

4. How does this cartoon relate to the First Amendment?

   _____

5. This cartoon was drawn and published in 1907. Why do you think all of the signers in the cartoon are men?

   _____

Teacher Notes
Amendments II Through X

Objectives

☆ Identify the rights listed in the Bill of Rights
☆ Identify symbols found in the cartoons
☆ Identify elements of irony and satire
☆ Identify cartoonists' messages
☆ Identify historical symbols
☆ Explain what symbols mean
☆ Recognize the meaning and subject of each cartoon
☆ Judge messages found in the cartoons

Vocabulary

bail	Money deposited with the court to get an arrested person temporarily released from jail on a promise to appear for trial
capital crime	Crimes punishable by death, such as murder or treason
common law	Laws dealing with private, not criminal or military, matters
due process	The legal proceedings established by a nation or state to protect individual rights and liberties
disparage	To discredit
enumeration	Determining the number of, the count
indictment	A formal accusation by a grand jury, charging a person with a crime after studying the evidence
infamous crime	Punishable by imprisonment
infringed	Encroach, or trespassed
jeopardy	Placing a person in great danger or peril
oath	A declaration to keep a promise or to tell the truth
seizure	The act of legally taking possession by force
warrant	A court order giving an officer legal authority to make an arrest, seizure or search
writ	Formal legal document ordering or prohibiting some action

The Bill of Rights

message

satire

symbols   *meaning*

Background Information

Even before the Constitution was adopted by all of the states, the debate began for a bill of rights that would guarantee personal liberties and freedoms for the citizens of the newly formed country. In a letter written on December 20, 1787, only three months after the Constitution was agreed upon by Congress to be sent to the states for ratification, Thomas Jefferson wrote to James Madison, "Let me add that a bill of rights is what the people are entitled to against every government on earth, general or particular, and what no government should refuse, or rest on inference."

The rights guaranteed in the Bill of Rights safeguard many of the freedoms that the colonists fought for in the Revolutionary War. Many of the freedoms that are guaranteed in the Bill of Rights were listed as grievances in the Declaration of Independence against King George III. The study of the Bill of Rights is important to every student so they know the foundation in understanding what their rights are as a citizen.

In this section students learn about the Second through Tenth Amendments in the Bill of Rights.

"I'm taking a poll, . . ."

The cartoon on is about the cherished American right to own guns, protected in the Second Amendment. It was been the Minute Men and citizen militias, along with a ragtag Continental Army that defeated the British. The framers of the Constitution wanted to protect citizens and their right to carry guns, safeguarding them against a government that was too strong. Only an armed citizenry could do that. This right had been the right of protestant Englishmen since the English Bill of Rights of 1689: The subjects, which are protestants, may have arms for their defence suitable to their conditions, and as allowed by law."

In this cartoon, a poll-taker knocks at the door to ask questions about the Second Amendment. Both people who live in the house are holding guns, unbeknownst to the poll-taker, illustrating the popularity of the Second Amendment with the "silent majority."

"I'd like to stay in your house for a few days with my platoon—we don't eat much."

The cartoon on page 98 refers to the Third Amendment. While this amendment probably doesn't mean much to Americans now, from 1765 until the end of the American Revolution British troops were stationed in the colonies. Various laws were passed to force the colonists to provide lodging and provisions for the soldiers. On March 28, 1774, Parliament passed the Quartering Act granting British soldiers the right to be housed in private citizens' homes, in inns and in public warehouses. The American colonists were outraged. In 1833, Justice Joseph Story summed up the Third Amendment when he wrote, "This provision speaks for itself. Its plain objective is to secure the perfect enjoyment of that great right of the common law, that a man's house shall be his own castle, privileged against all civil and military intrusion."

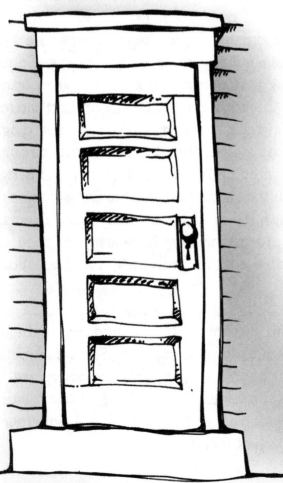

NSA

Under a series of laws passed in 1767, Parliamen gave broad powers to British customs office and their subordinates who were searchir homes and commercial buildings for smuggle goods. The officers were given writs of assi tance, giving them permission to search ar houses they chose, anytime, for any reason. No only could these customs officers search ar house they wished, the writs of assistance wei transferable to their assistants.

James Otis was a fiery orator in the America colonies and an able advocate for civil libertie Otis was asked to argue for the Boston me chants against the customs officers holding th writs. Though Otis lost the case, he eloquent outlined the elements that should be found in writ to safeguard people against an abuse of ci authority.

Otis said, "A man's house is his castle; and whil he is quiet, he is as well guarded as a prince in h castle . . . special writs may be granted on oat and probable suspicion . . . that an officer shou show probable ground; should take his oath of should do this before a magistrate; and that suc magistrate, if he thinks proper, should issue a sp cial warrant to a constable to search the places

Essentially, this cartoonist believes the Bus Administration, which ordered the Nation Security Agency (NSA) shortly after th September 11 attacks, to listen in on telephor conversations and read computer messages witl out a court order, violated American civil libe ties.

"All right, Spottie, . . ."

The cartoon on page 102 is about the Fifth Amendment. This amendment has three main clauses. The first clause guarantees that, except in military cases, no one can be held in jail for a crime that is punishable by death or imprisonment unless a grand jury evaluates the evidence presented to it and determines that there is enough evidence for a trial. (A grand jury is made up of 12 or more people.)

The second clause contains three parts. The first says a person cannot be tried for the same crime twice. The second says a defendant does not have to testify against himself. The third part of this clause has its roots in the Magna Carta of 1215. King John promised to give "due process of law" to all accused of crimes. All citizens are entitled to all courses of the law before the government can take away life, liberty or property.

ho-hum

I refuse to answer...

"Oh-oh–I should have gone for a jury trial."

The cartoon on page 104 is about the Sixth Amendment. The Sixth Amendment lays out eight specific rules for the judicial treatment of people who are charged with a crime. Anyone charged with a crime has a right to a speedy trial. The trial has to be public so nothing secret can go on unseen by the citizens. The jury has to be impartial or made up of people who do not have an opinion about the crime that had been committed or the accused. The trial has to take place in the area where the crime was committed. The accused has to be informed of the charges. The person on trial has to be able to see the people who were witnesses in the case. The accused has to have a means by which to call witnesses for his own defense. And lastly, the person accused of the crime has a right to an attorney.

In this cartoon, the cat is clearly worried that the mouse is going to hold the fact that he is a cat against him and he will not get a fair trial. The cat truly believes that he will not get a fair and impartial trial.

"If that doesn't work, there is always the People's Court on TV!"

The cartoon on page 106, refers to the Seventh Amendment provides that private citizens are guaranteed a trial by jury for cases involving more than $20. That doesn't seem like much, but in 1791, when this amendment was ratified, $20 represented about 40 days' pay for the average American.

According to the Bureau of Labor Statistics, the average pay in 2001 was $36,214. An additional activity might be to have your students' calculate what 40 days' pay for today's average American worker would be.

"I sentence you to one hour of listening to Barry Manilow's greatest hits!"

The Eighth Amendment represents another safeguard in the Bill of Rights against overzealous and unreasonable treatment of citizens by the court. This amendment had its origins in the English Bill of Rights of 1689 and is taken from that document nearly word for word. "That excessive bail ought not to be required, nor excessive fines, imposed; nor cruel and unusual punishment inflicted."

In Stack v. Boyle, Chief Justice Vinson defined what the Supreme Court meant by *excessive bail*. "The right to release before trial is conditioned upon the accused's giving adequate assurance that he will stand trial and submit to sentence if found guilty ... Like the ancient practice of securing oaths of responsible persons to stand as sureties for the accused, the modern practice of requiring a bail bond or the deposit of a sum of money subject to forfeiture serves as additional assurance of the presence of an accused. Bail set at a figure higher than an amount reasonably calculated to fulfill this purpose is excessive under the Eighth Amendment."

The meaning of the term *cruel and unusual* ha[s] changed from one generation to another. At th[e] time this amendment was written, the framer[s] knew many punishments that we would no[t] consider cruel and unusual. For instance, a pe[r]son could be sentenced to stand all day in th[e] stocks, a wooden frame made in two parts s[o] when it closed it fit around the neck and wrist[s]. Part of the punishment was the discomfort [of] being in the stocks and not being able to mov[e] about, as well as the humiliation of being seen th[is] way in public.

In the cartoon on page 108, the cartoonist [is] passing judgment on a Colorado judge's punish[]ment for people found guilty of violating a noi[se] pollution statute. In most cases, the peop[le] charged with violating the city ordinance we[re] cruising around the streets of the small tow[n] playing rap music blaring from their car radio[s]. Fort Lupton, Colorado, Judge Paul Sacco se[n]tenced violators to listening to one hour of mus[ic] sung by Dolly Parton, Karen Carpenter or Bar[ry] Manilow.

"This is none of your business."

Justice William O. Douglas described the Ninth Amendment as protecting the "freedom of choice in the basic decisions of one's life respecting marriage, divorce, procreation, contraception, and the education and upbringing of children."

This amendment was born out of the fear the Americans had of tyrannical government. The colonists had just fought a long and costly war to rid themselves of the power of a king. They didn't want a new government to take the king's place. Why switch one tyrant for another?

The writers of the Bill of Rights feared that if the rights weren't spelled out in the Constitution, the federal government would assume jurisdiction. This amendment was written to make sure that wouldn't happen.

In the cartoon on page 110, the couple getting married is telling Uncle Sam, who represents the federal government in this cartoon, that marriage laws are none of the federal government's business.

"Stay out of our schools with your rules!"

The debate over who should have more power, the states or the federal government, was at the heart of the Constitutional Convention of 1787 and continues to this day. This amendment was written to guarantee that the federal government could not usurp power from the states by claiming powers not delegated to it by the Constitution. The Constitution leaves it to the states to make laws about marriage, divorce, education, zoning, public health, driving regulations and state roads, among others.

The cartoon on page 112 suggests that the No Child Left Behind Law that provides rules for every public school in America is unconstitutional because the Tenth Amendment says that is an area under the preview of the states as schools are not specifically mentioned as being a federal responsibility.

Suggested Lesson Plan

1. Share the "Words to Look For" list on page 88 with your students. Invite them to look for the words on the list as they read through the "Bill of Rights" handout (pages 94-95).
2. Share the text of Amendments II through X with your students.
3. Ask students to explain each of the nine Amendments in their own words.
4. Use the editorial cartoon handouts to start class discussions about what each one of the Amendments mean.
5. Use the "Rights Review" handouts on pages 114-116 to check the students' understanding of the Amendments in the Bill of Rights.

states' powers

federal powers

Bill of Rights

Amendment I

Congress shall make no law respecting an establishment of religion, or prohibiting the free exercise thereof; or abridging the freedom of speech, or of the press; or the right of the people peaceably to assemble, and to petition the government for a redress of grievances.

Amendment II

A well-regulated militia, being necessary to the security of a free state, the right of the people to keep and bear arms shall not be infringed.

Amendment III

No soldier shall, in time of peace be quartered in any house, without the consent of the owner, nor in time of war, but in a manner to be prescribed by law.

Amendment IV

The right of the people to be secure in their persons, houses, papers, and effects, against unreasonable searches and seizures, shall not be violated, and no warrants shall issue, but upon probable cause, supported by oath or affirmation, and particularly describing the place to be searched, and the persons or things to be seized.

Amendment V

No person shall be held to answer for a capital, or otherwise infamous crime, unless on a presentment or indictment of a grand jury, except in cases arising in the land or naval forces, or in the militia, when in actual service in time of war or public danger; nor shall any person be subject for the same offense to be twice put in jeopardy of life or limb; nor shall be compelled in any criminal case to be a witness against himself, nor be deprived of life, liberty, or property, without due process of law; nor shall private property be taken for public use, without just compensation.

...in order to form...

Amendment VI

In all criminal prosecutions, the accused shall enjoy the right to a speedy and public trial, by an impartial jury of the state and district wherein the crime shall have been committed, which district shall have been previously ascertained by law, and to be informed of the nature and cause of the accusation; to be confronted with the witnesses against him; to have compulsory process for obtaining witnesses in his favor, and to have the assistance of counsel for his defense.

Amendment VII

In suits at common law, where the value in controversy shall exceed twenty dollars, the right of trial by jury shall be preserved, and no fact tried by a jury, shall be otherwise reexamined in any court of the United States, than according to the rules of the common law.

Amendment VIII

Excessive bail shall not be required, nor excessive fines imposed, nor cruel and unusual punishments inflicted.

Amendment IX

The enumeration in the Constitution, of certain rights, shall not be construed to deny or disparage others retained by the people.

Amendment X

The powers not delegated to the United States by the Constitution, nor prohibited by it to the states, are reserved to the states respectively, or to the people.

A more perfect Union

Name _____

"I'm taking a poll, Sir. Are you for or against gun control?"

By Wayne Stayskal

Study the cartoon, then complete page 97.

Name _____

"I'm taking a poll, Sir. Are you for or against gun control?"

By Wayne Stayskal

Study the cartoon on page 96, then write the letter of the correct words to complete each sentence.

_____ 1. This editorial cartoonist is "drawing" attention to
        a. the First Amendment.
        b. the Second Amendment.
        c. the Third Amendment.

_____ 2. The man at the door has a clipboard in his hand to
        a. take notes about the people with whom he talks.
        b. record the answers for the poll he is taking.
        c. gathering signatures for a petition he is circulating.

_____ 3. The couple in the cartoon are most likely
        a. in favor of gun control.
        b. against gun control.
        c. having a water pistol fight interrupted by a knock on the door.

Bonus: Explain how you chose your answer for question 3. What clues in the cartoon led you to an answer?

_____

_____

_____

"I'd like to stay in your house for a few days with my platoon— we don't eat much!"

Study the cartoon, then complete page 99.

Illustration by Bron Smith.

"I'd like to stay in your house for a few days with my platoon— we don't eat much!"

Study the cartoon on page 98, then write the letter of the correct words to complete each statement.

_____ 1. The cartoonist is "drawing" attention to:
        a. the Second Amendment.
        b. the Third Amendment.
        c. the Fourth Amendment.

_____ 2. The man in the vehicle is a
        a. soldier.
        b. driving instructor.
        c. neighbor.

_____ 3. This amendment was written
        a. to protect a person's home from outside intrusion by the government.
        b. agrees with the statement that "a person's home is their castle."
        c. both answers "a" and "b" are correct.

Bonus: When was this right a deep concern among the American people?

_____

_____

_____

NSA

By Mike Keefe

Study the cartoon, then complete page 101.

NSA Eavesdropping © 2007. All rights reserved. Used with the permission of Mike Keefe and dePixon Studios.

Name _____

NSA

By Mike Keefe

Study the cartoon on page 100, then write the letter of the correct words to complete each statement.

_____ 1. The cartoonist is "drawing" attention to
     a. the Second Amendment.
     b. the Third Amendment.
     c. the Fourth Amendment.

_____ 2. The woman in the cartoon is
     a. a television anchor woman.
     b. the Statue of Liberty.
     c. a secret agent.

_____ 3. The woman in the cartoon is holding
     a. a microphone.
     b. a listening device.
     c. both answers "a" and "b" are correct.

_____ 4. According to the cartoonist, our civil liberties were
     a. smashed.
     b. upheld.
     c. strengthened.

"All right, Spottie, bark once for 'yes,' and twice for 'no' and five times if you wish to take the 5th."

Study the cartoon, then complete page 103.

"All right Spottie, bark once for 'yes', twice for 'no' and five times if you wish to take the 5th."

TLC10541 Copyright © Teaching & Learning Company, Carthage, IL 62321-00

"All right, Spottie, bark once for 'yes,' and twice for 'no' and five times if you wish to take the 5th."

Cartoon by Dan Rosandich

Study the cartoon on page 102, then write the letter of the correct words to complete each statement.

____ 1. The cartoonist is "drawing" attention to
    a. the Fourth Amendment.
    b. the Fifth Amendment.
    c. the Sixth Amendment.

____ 2. The dog in the cartoon is
    a. in the witness chair of a courtroom.
    b. in dog obedience training.
    c. in school.

____ 3. The dog is being asked to testify
    a. as a witness.
    b. in a case against another dog.
    c. on his own behalf.

bark! bark! bark! bark! bark!

Bonus: Explain your last answer.

_____

_____

_____

_____

Name _____

"Oh-oh—I should have gone for a jury trial."

By Mike Twohy

Study the cartoon, then complete page 105.

TLC10541 Copyright © Teaching & Learning Company, Carthage, IL 62321-00

"Oh-oh—I should have gone for a jury trial."

Cartoon by Mike Twohy

Study the cartoon on page 104, then write the letter of the correct words to complete each statement.

____ 1. The cartoonist is "drawing" attention to
   a. the Fourth Amendment.
   b. the Fifth Amendment.
   c. the Sixth Amendment.

____ 2. The cat in the cartoon is
   a. is scared because the mouse looks angry.
   b. does not want a mouse as a judge.
   c. is upset because he swallowed a hair ball.

____ 3. The cat wants a
   a. a jury of his peers.
   b. an impartial jury.
   c. both answers "a" and "b" are correct.

Name _____

"If that doesn't work, there is always the *People's Court* on *TV!*"

Study the cartoon, then complete page 107.

Illustration by Bron Smith.

"If that doesn't work, there is always the *People's Court* on *TV!*"

Study the cartoon on page 106, then write the letter of the correct words to **complete each statement.**

_____ 1. The cartoonist is "drawing" attention to
   a. the Fifth Amendment.
   b. the Sixth Amendment.
   c. the Seventh Amendment.

_____ 2. The woman in the cartoon is holding
   a. a $20 bill.
   b. a dry cleaning bill for $20.
   c. her marriage license.

_____ 3. The woman is guaranteed a court trial in civil court because
   a. the amount is over $1000.
   b. the amount is $20 or more.
   c. any amount is important enough for a civil trial.

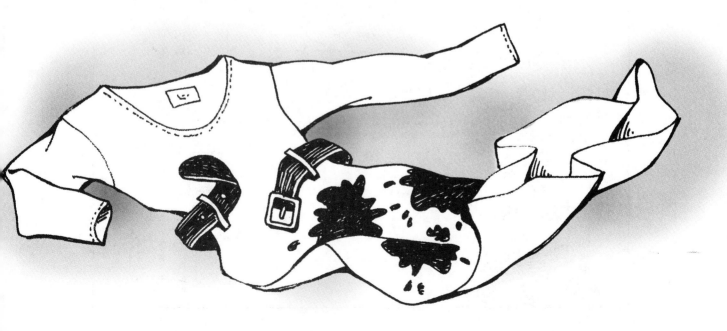

"I sentence you to listening to one hour of Barry Manilow's greatest hits."

Study the cartoon, then complete page 109.

Illustration by Bron Smith.

Name _____

"I sentence you to listening to one hour of Barry Manilow's greatest hits."

Study the cartoon on page 108, then write the letter of the correct words to complete each statement.

_____ 1. The cartoonist is "drawing" attention to
        a. the Eighth Amendment.
        b. the Ninth Amendment.
        c. the Tenth Amendment.

_____ 2. The defendant in this case thinks the punishment is
        a. groovy and hip.
        b. far out.
        c. cruel.

Bonus: Name a punishment that has been used in America's past that we now think of as cruel or unusual.

_____

_____

_____

_____

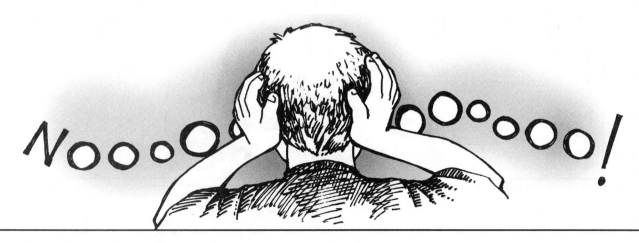

Name _____

"This is none of your business."

Study the cartoon, then complete page 111.

Illustration by Bron Smith.

Name _____

"This is none of your business,"

Study the cartoon on page 110, then write the letter of the correct words to complete each statement.

_____ 1. The cartoonist is "drawing" attention to
      a. the eighth Amendment.
      b. the Ninth Amendment.
      c. the Tenth Amendment.

_____ 2. The couple in the cartoon are
      a. getting married.
      b. posing for a picture.
      c. running for office.

_____ 3. Uncle Sam in this cartoon represents
      a. the federal government.
      b. the state government.
      c. the people.

Name _____

"Stay out of our schools with your rules!"

Study the cartoon, then complete page 113.

Illustration by Bron Smith.

"Stay out of our schools with your rules!"

Study the cartoon on page 112, then write the letter of the correct words to complete each statement.

_____ 1. The cartoonist is "drawing" attention to
   a. the Eighth Amendment.
   b. the Ninth Amendment.
   c. the Tenth Amendment.

_____ 2. The person in the school is
   a. a parent.
   b. a teacher.
   c. a student.

_____ 3. Uncle Sam represents
   a. the federal government.
   b. President George W. Bush.
   c. both answers "a" and "b" are correct.

_____ 4. According to the cartoonist, NCLB is
   a. unconstitutional.
   b. within the federal government's authority.
   c. something students should think about.

Name _____

Rights Review

Place the amendment number next to the right guaranteed by the Bill of Rights.

_____ 1. The right to a trial by jury in criminal cases

_____ 2. The right to call witnesses in one's defense at a trial

_____ 3. Freedom of the press

_____ 4. Not to testify against oneself

_____ 5. The right to be informed of why you are being arrested

_____ 6. Freedom of religion

_____ 7. The right to a trial by jury in civil cases of $20

_____ 8. No excessive bail

_____ 9. The right to bear arms

_____ 10. Protection from unreasonable search and seizure

114

Rights Review

Place the amendment number next to the right guaranteed by the Bill of Rights.

_____ 1. Right to a speedy trial

_____ 2. Freedom of speech

_____ 3. No cruel or unusual punishment

_____ 4. The right to confront witnesses

_____ 5. The right not to quarter soldiers in your home

_____ 6. Cannot be tried for the same crime twice

_____ 7. The right to assembly

_____ 8. The right to a trial in the district the crime occurred

_____ 9. Cannot be deprived of life, liberty or property without just compensation

_____ 10. The right to redress of grievances

Name _____

Rights Review

1. Name the five rights guaranteed in the First Amendment.

_____

_____

_____

_____

2. Name three of the five rights guaranteed in the Fifth Amendment.

_____

_____

_____

3. What three rights are enumerated in the Eighth Amendment?

_____

_____

_____

☆☆☆ Bill of Rights Scrapping ☆☆☆

Objective

↳ To help students understand the Bill of Rights. They will do this by identifying current events that reveal Civil Rights "violations" and maintain them in a series of designated "pockets" to display. Other more activist roles include addressing the contemporary issues with state representatives, etc.

Background Information

The first 10 Amendments to the United States Constitution are the Bill of Rights. James Madison introduced them in 1789 during the First United States Congress. In 1791 they were ratified. The Bill of Rights plays a central role in American law and government. It remains a fundamental symbol of the freedoms and culture of the nation. The purposes of these Amendments were to limit the powers of the federal government and protect the rights of all citizens, residents and visitors in the United States territories. Among the rights guaranteed are the freedoms of speech, press, assembly, religion, right to keep and bear arms, petition, unreasonable search and seizure, cruel and unusual punishment and so on. The Bill of Rights also restricts the power of Congress by prohibiting the government from depriving any person of the right of life, liberty or property without due process of the law. In criminal cases this includes speedy trials, indictments of grand juries and impartial juries.

One or more students

Materials

plywood board (12" x 24" x 1/8" wide)
index cards 3" x 5"
clear plastic folder sleeves—top loading, three per board
stapler and staples
double-sided tape
black marker
spray paint of any color choice

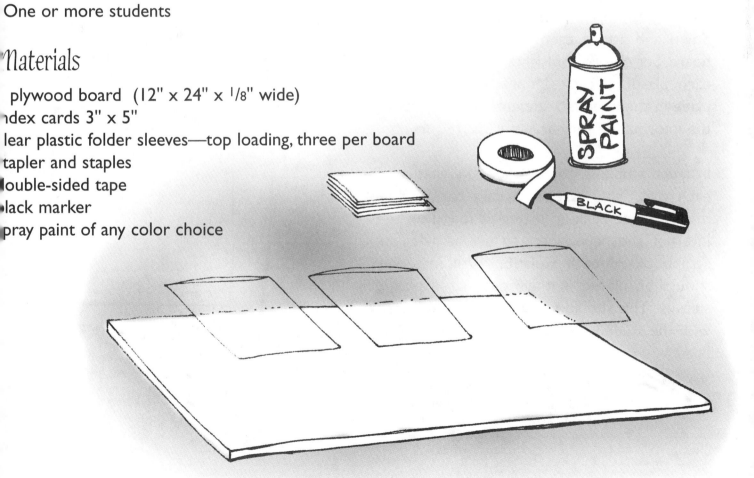

Directions

1. Discuss the Bill of Rights and its importance. Explain that in this project students will be required to watch national and local news, read newspapers and the Internet to find current topics on civil rights and various violations. Instruct them to cut out all items and bring them to class. The class will vote on three civil rights cases they have located and are interested in following for the duration of the cases.

2. Write down the three Bill of Rights the students will focus on index cards. Make a display board by spray painting the plywood panel with your desired color.

   Place the painted board in a horizontal position. Set three clear top-loading plastic sleeves 5" from the top of the panel. (Figure 1)

3. Hold each sleeve in place and slip a stapler between the plastic sheets. Press the stapler down and attach each plastic sleeve to the board. Set one Bill of Rights index card above each plastic sleeve. Mount in a prominent place in the room so students have access to the information they accumulate. (Figure 2)

4. Instruct students to describe the status of each civil rights case on a daily basis. They must provide back-up materials found on the Internet and newspapers to use as a log or scrapbook of each violation. All materials should be placed in their designated plastic sleeves. This should invite dialog and concern with the students.

5. Encourage students to take an active role i lawmaking and be aware of their civil rights a well as that of others in the country. Hav them enact a writing campaign to their cor gressmen and representatives, judges an councilmen. They should use the clippings a reference for support.

Figure 1

Figure 2

118

✩✩✩ Amendment Card Game ✩✩✩

Objective

↻ A matching card game to help students gain a better understanding of the Amendments and the Constitution.

Background Information

The Amendment Card Game is played in the style of the popular card game, Go Fish! This fun game reinforces previously studied information. With some variations it may also be used to introduce new material on a myriad of subjects. In the Amendments Card Game, students will be exposed to various changes and modifications of the Constitution. It challenges students to gain an understanding of the Constitution, perspectives of the times and people in U.S. history.

Two to four players

Materials

markers
laminator/clear, self-adhesive paper

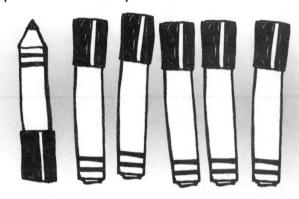

Directions

1. Provide students with background information about the Amendments. Explain to them that the Founding Fathers understood that the Constitution would require alteration and evaluation of the laws as time went on.

2. Ask students to define the term *Amendment*. Discuss some of the well-known Amendments that were added to the Constitution later, such as the Thirteenth Amendment. Ask how it changed the minds of people and the course of history.

3. Divide the class into teams of two to six students each. Make four copies of each of the Amendments (pages 121-123) for each team. Ask volunteers to color and cut out the card section and laminate to make a deck of cards.

4. Explain that this game is played like Go Fish! Ask volunteers who have played this game to model one round as the rules are explained.

5. When play ends, ask students which Amendments helped them win the game with the matches. Have them discuss the Amendments and encourage other students to dialog.

Rules

1. The main object of the game is for players to get rid of all their cards by creating matches.

2. Five cards are dealt to each student in the game.

3. Player 1 looks at his or her card, chooses a card and asks Player 2 for a matching one. For example: Do you have the Fifteenth Amendment? Player 1 cannot ask for a card that is not in his or her own hand.

4. If Player 2 has the card, he or she must give it to Player 1.

5. If Player 2 does not have the card, he or she says, "Go Amendments!" And Player 1 must draw a card from the deck placed in the middle of the players.

6. The game continues until a player runs out of cards or there are no cards left to draw from the pile. The player with the most matches wins.

Go Amendments! Playing Card Images

First Amendment: Addresses the rights of freedom of religion, freedom of speech, freedom of the press, freedom of assembly and freedom of petition.

Second Amendment: To keep and bear arms.

Third Amendment: Prohibits the government from using private homes as quarters for soldiers without the consent of the owners.

Fourth Amendment: Guards against searches, arrests, and seizures of property without a specific warrant or a "probable cause."

Fifth Amendment: Forbids trial for a major crime except after indictment by a grand jury; prohibits double jeopardy (repeated trials), forbids punishment without due process of law.

Sixth Amendment: Guarantees a speedy public trial.

Seventh Amendment: Assures trial by jury in civil cases.

Eighth Amendment: Forbids cruel and unusual punishment.

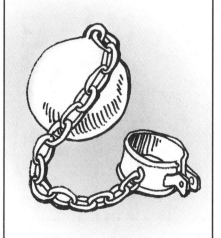

Ninth Amendment: The people have rights beyond the scope of the Constitution.

Go Amendments! Playing Card Images

Tenth Amendment: Provides that the states are "reserved to the states respectively, or to the people."

Eleventh Amendment: Clarifies judicial power over foreign nationals, and limits ability of citizens to sue states.

Twelfth Amendment (1804): Changes the method of presidential elections with members of the electoral college casting separate ballots for President and Vice President.

Thirteenth Amendment (1865): Abolishes slavery.

Fourteenth Amendment (1868): Defines citizens' privileges or immunities and rights to due process and the equal protection of the law.

Fifteenth Amendment (1870): Forbids the use of a citizen's race, color or previous status as a slave as a qualification for voting.

Sixteenth Amendment (1913): Authorizes unapportioned taxes on income.

Seventeenth Amendment (1913): Establishes the election of senators.

Eighteenth Amendment (1919): Prohibits the manufacturing, importing and exporting of alcoholic beverages.

Go Amendments! Playing Card Images

Nineteenth Amendment (1920): Prohibits forbidding any citizen to vote due to their sex.

Twentieth Amendment (1933): Changes details of congressional and presidential terms and presidential succession.

Twenty-First Amendment (1933): Repeals Eighteenth Amendment. Permits states to prohibit the importation of alcoholic beverages.

Twenty-Second Amendment (1951): Limits two terms for the President.

Twenty-Third Amendment (1961): Grants presidential electors to the District of Columbia.

Twenty-Fourth Amendment (1964): Prohibits the payment of a tax as a qualification for voting for federal officials.

Twenty-Fifth Amendment (1967): Provides for temporary removal of President, and provides for replacement of the Vice President.

Twenty-Sixth Amendment (1971): Prohibits the federal government and the states from forbidding any citizen the right to vote if 18 years or older.

Twenty-Seventh Amendment (1992): Limits congressional pay raises.

 # Political Cartoon Triptych

Objective

☆ Establish which aspect in the Constitution political cartoons portray.

Background Information

After careful study of the political cartoons, students will make their own political cartoon triptyc[h]
They will do this by researching historical cartoons which mirror or represent the topics feature[d]
Students will then make a standing display triptych of the political cartoons, old and new. Discussi[on]
topics include: Why were the cartoons chosen? What was their significance? How concepts diff[er]
from today?

*Individual or group project

Materials

Internet access
ribbon 1" wide by 40" long
white glue

6 sheets of 11" x 14" poster board
masking tape

Directions

1. Students should have prior knowledge of the Constitution, Articles, Amendments and Bill of Rights. Direct them to choose a contemporary political cartoon. Copy the cartoon on 8½" x 11" paper.

2. Students will locate two additional historic political cartoons, which match the theme of their contemporary cartoon. A good resource to use is the Library of Congress, Prints and Photos Division at http://www.loc.gov/rr/ print/catalog.html. Print the new images at 8½" x 11".

3. Cut three sheets of poster board to 11" x 14". Lay them side-by-side.

Figure 1

Cut two 12" strips of ribbon and saturate with glue. Lay the ribbons down on the two middle seams and let dry. (Figure 1)

Take the additional three pieces of poster board and trim ¹/₃" on all sides.

Cut 12 3" strips of ribbon. Dab the edges of four of these ribbons with glue. Place one ribbon at an angle on the corner edge of the board and flip the glued ribbon edge over to the other side. These ribbon corner edges will be used to hold the cartoons in place. Do this with all corners for each board. Let dry. (Figure 2)

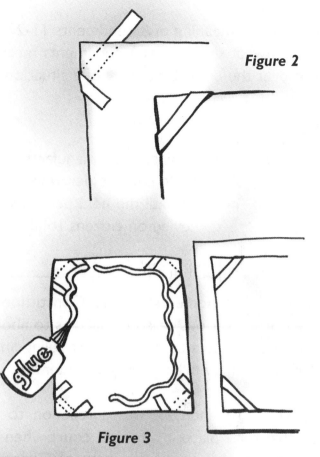

Figure 2

Flip the boards with the ribbon corners over to reveal the glued ends. Saturate each back board with glue and place each board centered on top of each of the three panels. Let dry. (Figure 3)

Figure 3

Slip the political cartoons into each ribbon edge of each panel. Flip the triptych over and decorate. Let the display stand by slightly folding the two outer ends. (Figure 4)

Figure 4

Teacher Notes
Amendments XI Through XXVII

Objectives

☆ Identify the meaning of Amendments 11-27
☆ Explain what the various Amendments mean
☆ Interpret the constitutionality of a situation

Vocabulary

Prohibition   The banning of the manufacture and sale of alcohol
lame duck   An elected officeholder who did not win or did not run in the last election but is st[ill] in office until the next person who was elected to the office takes the office
poll tax   A tax levied on citizens to allow them to vote

Background Information

The last 17 Amendments to the Constitution came about for various reasons: such as to abolish slavery, overrule a Supreme Court ruling and improve upon the workings of government.

The Eleventh Amendment was a reaction to a lawsuit that took place in a federal court when a South Carolina man sued the state of Georgia, Chisholm v. Georgia, 1793. The states reacted swiftly fearing that others could do the same unless a constitutional amendment prohibited it. In less than two years the Eleventh Amendment was ratified.

The Twelfth Amendment was intended to fix the way electors voted for President and Vice President of the United States. In the election of 1800, Thomas Jefferson and Aaron Burr, both of the Democratic-Republican party, each received 73 electoral votes. One was required to have a majority of the electoral votes cast. The election eventually ended up being settled in the House of Representatives. The Twelfth Amendment made it clear that electors were to vote for a candidate for President and vote for a candidate for Vice President.

The Thirteenth Amendment abolished the instit[u]tion of slavery which had remained protected [by] the Constitution. In fact, the importation [of] slaves was guaranteed in the Constitution un[til] 1808. After 1808, a series of laws and compr[o]mises tried to maintain a balance of free and sla[ve] states. After the Civil War, the country sought [to] legally and constitutionally abolish slave[ry] through this amendment.

The Fourteenth Amendment was ratified to gra[nt] former slaves the full benefits and rights [of] American citizenship.

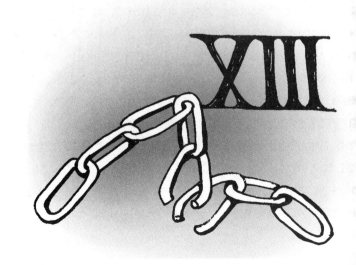

126

VOTE

fter the Civil War, there were intense discrimi-tion and anti-slavery prejudices. People of lor were being turned out of their homes and eprived of many of their rights, including their ght to vote. The Fifteenth Amendment was rat-ed as a way to ensure that race, color and the atus of someone as a former slave could not be ed as a reason to keep that person from voting.

he Sixteenth Amendment gave the federal gov-nment the power to tax incomes.

he Seventeenth Amendment was ratified to ake United States senators elected directly by e people instead of the state legislatures. This nendment was passed to thwart one of the iticisms that many parts of the Constitution ere undemocratic and that the framers were ary of general elections by the people. By the ne this Amendment was passed, some thought at the legislative process to elect senators was rrupt and that the system did not reflect the ll of the people.

The Eighteenth Amendment was ratified after years of debate and campaigning against the evils of alcohol. The temperance movement started in the early part of the nineteenth century and by 1855, a little more than a third of the 31 states had laws on the books that prohibited the con-sumption of alcohol. After the Civil War there was an increase in the number of taverns and saloons and the ills associated with them such as gambling, public drunkenness and disorderly con-duct. There was a resurgence of the temperance movement led by people like Carry Nation who wanted a national ban on the consumption of alcohol. The Anti-Saloon League took up the fight for a national prohibition. In the election of 1915, candidates who had endorsed the Anti-Saloon League platform swept into Congress.

The Nineteenth Amendment expanded the fran-chise to include women. Women had campaigned since the Seneca Falls Convention in 1848 for the right to vote. After the Civil War, women like Elizabeth Cady Stanton and Susan B. Anthony took up the fight again.

Susan B. Anthony

The Twentieth Amendment attempts to solve the lame duck presidency. A lame duck is used for a person who has not been re-elected but is still in office. When the presidential election took place in November and the new President was not inaugurated until March there was a much longer time for a President to be "lame duck." The Twentieth Amendment shortened the period of time between the election and the inauguration.

The Twenty-First Amendment repealed the Eighteenth Amendment making it legal once again in the United States to produce and distribute alcohol.

The Twenty-Second Amendment codified what had been precedent that a President only serve two terms. From George Washington until Franklin D. Roosevelt, no President had served more than two terms. Roosevelt was elected to an unprecedented four terms as President. After Roosevelt's death, Congress determined that Washington's two-term self-imposed rule should be the law of the land.

The Twenty-Third Amendment extended voting rights for the District of Columbia electors for President. This meant that in presidential elections, Washington, D.C., would have representation in the electoral college.

The Twenty-Fourth Amendment forbade states from applying a poll tax for people to vote. The poll tax had been a way for states to keep African-Americans from voting.

The Twenty-Fifth Amendment was passed after the death of President Kennedy. It was the intent of Congress to codify who would become President after a President's death and in the event that the Vice President was also incapacitated or dead. The Amendment defines the line of succession.

The Twenty-Sixth Amendment was a reaction to the call from 18-year-olds who were being asked to fight and die in the Vietnam War but were not legally able to vote in presidential elections. The Amendment extended the franchise to 18-year-olds.

The Twenty-Seventh Amendment was a long time in ratification. It was first proposed in September 25, 1789, but was not ratified until May 7, 1992, a whopping 74,003 days later. This amendment states that a sitting Congress cannot increase their own pay, that is, it does not go into effect until the next Congress is seated.

Suggested Lesson Plan

1. Share the lesson objectives with students.
2. Explain the vocabulary and background information.
3. Invite students to read Amendments 11-27 on pages 129-135.
4. Invite your students to read and answer the questions on pages 136-137 covering the material.

The following text is the original language from the Constitution. The passages that are underlined were later changed by the Amendment process.

Amendments XI Through XXVII

Amendment XI

January 8, 1798

The judicial power of the United States shall not be construed to extend to any suit in law or equity, commenced or prosecuted against one of the United States by citizens of another state, or by citizens or subjects of any foreign state.

Amendment XII

September 25, 1804

The electors shall meet in their respective states and vote by ballot for President and Vice President, one of whom, at least, shall not be an inhabitant of the same state with themselves; they shall name in their ballots the person voted for as President, and in distinct ballots the person voted for as Vice President, and they shall make distinct lists of all persons voted for as President, and of all persons voted for as Vice President, and of the number of votes for each, which lists they shall sign and certify, and transmit sealed to the seat of the government of the United States, directed to the President of the Senate;—The President of the Senate shall, in the presence of the Senate and House of Representatives, open all the certificates and the votes shall then be counted;—the person having the greatest number of votes for President, shall be the President, if such number be a majority of the whole number of electors appointed; and if no person have such majority, then from the persons having the highest numbers not exceeding three on the list of those voted for as President, the House of Representatives shall choose immediately, by ballot, the President. But in choosing the President, the votes shall be taken by states, the representation from each state having one vote; a quorum for this purpose shall consist of a member or members from two-thirds of the states, and a majority of all the states shall be necessary to a choice. And if the House of Representatives shall not choose a President whenever the right of choice shall devolve upon them, before the fourth day of March next following, then the Vice President shall act as President, as in the case of the death or other constitutional disability of the President.—The person having the greatest number of votes as Vice President, shall be the Vice President, if such number be a majority of the whole number of electors appointed, and if no person have a majority, then from the two highest numbers on the list, the Senate shall choose the Vice President; a quorum for the purpose shall consist of two-thirds of the whole number of senators, and a majority of the whole number shall be necessary to a choice. But no person constitutionally ineligible to the office of President shall be eligible to that of Vice President of the United States.

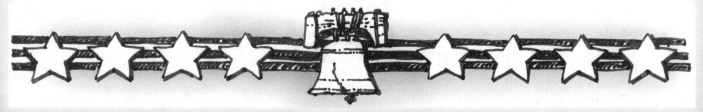

Amendment XIII

December 18, 1865

Section 1. Neither slavery nor involuntary servitude, except as a punishment for crime where-of the party shall have been duly convicted, shall exist within the United States, or any place subject to their jurisdiction.

Section 2. Congress shall have power to enforce this article by appropriate legislation.

Amendment XIV

July 28, 1868

Section 1. All persons born or naturalized in the United States, and subject to the jurisdiction thereof, are citizens of the United States and of the state wherein they reside. No state shall make or enforce any law which shall abridge the privileges or immunities of citizens of the United States; nor shall any state deprive any person of life, liberty, or property, without due process of law; nor deny to any person within its jurisdiction the equal protection of the laws.

Section 2. Representatives shall be apportioned among the several states according to their respective numbers, counting the whole number of persons in each state, excluding Indians not taxed. But when the right to vote at any election for the choice of electors for President and Vice President of the United States, representatives in Congress, the executive and judicial officers of a state, or the members of the legislature thereof, is denied to any of the <u>male</u> inhabitants of such state, <u>being twenty-one years of age</u>, and citizens of the United States, or in any way abridged, except for participation in rebellion, or other crime, the basis of representation therein shall be reduced in the proportion which the number of such male citizens shall bear to the whole number of male citizens twenty-one years of age in such state.

Section 3. No person shall be a senator or representative in Congress, or elector of President and Vice President, or hold any office, civil or military, under the United States, or under any state, who, having previously taken an oath, as a member of Congress, or as an officer of the United States, or as a member of any state legislature, or as an executive or judicial officer of any state, to support the Constitution of the United States, shall have engaged in insurrection or rebellion against the same, or given aid or comfort to the enemies thereof. But Congress may by a vote of two-thirds of each House, remove such disability.

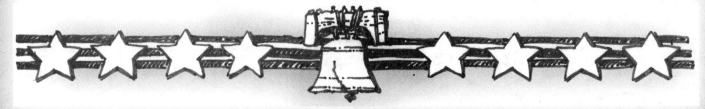

Section 4. The validity of the public debt of the United States, authorized by law, including debts incurred for payment of pensions and bounties for services in suppressing insurrection or rebellion, shall not be questioned. But neither the United States nor any state shall assume or pay any debt or obligation incurred in aid of insurrection or rebellion against the United States, or any claim for the loss or emancipation of any slave; but all such debts, obligations and claims shall be held illegal and void.

Section 5. The Congress shall have power to enforce, by appropriate legislation, the provisions of this article.

Amendment XV

March 30, 1870

Section 1. The right of citizens of the United States to vote shall not be denied or abridged by the United States or by any state on account of race, color, or previous condition of servitude.

Section 2. The Congress shall have power to enforce this article by appropriate legislation.

Amendment XVI

February 25, 1913

The Congress shall have power to lay and collect taxes on incomes, from whatever source derived, without apportionment among the several states, and without regard to any census or enumeration.

Amendment XVII

May 31, 1913

The Senate of the United States shall be composed of two senators from each state, elected by the people thereof, for six years; and each senator shall have one vote. The electors in each state shall have the qualifications requisite for electors of the most numerous branch of the state legislatures.

When vacancies happen in the representation of any state in the Senate, the executive authority of such state shall issue writs of election to fill such vacancies: *Provided*, that the legislature of any state may empower the executive thereof to make temporary appointments until the people fill the vacancies by election as the legislature may direct.

This amendment shall not be so construed as to affect the election or term of any senator chosen before it becomes valid as part of the Constitution.

Amendment XVIII

January 29, 1919

Section 1. After one year from the ratification of this article the manufacture, sale, or transportation of intoxicating liquors within, the importation thereof into, or the exportation thereof from the United States and all territory subject to the jurisdiction thereof for beverage purposes is hereby prohibited.

Section 2. The Congress and the several states shall have concurrent power to enforce this article by appropriate legislation.

Section 3. This article shall be inoperative unless it shall have been ratified as an amendment to the Constitution by the legislatures of the several states, as provided in the Constitution, within seven years from the date of the submission hereof to the states by the Congress.

Amendment XIX

August 26, 1920

Section 1. The right of citizens of the United States to vote shall not be denied or abridged by the United States or by any state on account of sex.

Section 2. Congress shall have power to enforce this article by appropriate legislation.

Amendment XX

February 6, 1933

Section 1. The terms of the President and Vice President shall end at noon on the 20th day of January, and the terms of senators and representatives at noon on the third day of January, of the years in which such terms would have ended if this article had not been ratified; and the terms of their successors shall then begin.

Section 2. The Congress shall assemble at least once in every year, and such meeting shall begin at noon on the third day of January, unless they shall by law appoint a different day.

Section 3. If, at the time fixed for the beginning of the term of the President, the President elect shall have died, the Vice President elect shall become President. If a President shall not have been chosen before the time fixed for the beginning of his term, or if the President elect shall have failed to qualify, then the Vice President elect shall act as President until a President shall have qualified; and the Congress may by law provide for the case wherein neither a President elect nor a Vice President elect shall have qualified, declaring who shall then act as President, or the manner in which one who is to act shall be selected, and such person shall act accordingly until a President or Vice President shall have qualified.

Section 4. The Congress may by law provide for the case of the death of any of the persons from whom the House of Representatives may choose a President whenever the right of choice shall have devolved upon them, and for the case of the death of any of the persons from whom the Senate may choose a Vice President whenever the right of choice shall have devolved upon them.

Section 5. Sections 1 and 2 shall take effect on the 15th day of October following the ratification of this article.

Section 6. This article shall be inoperative unless it shall have been ratified as an amendment to the Constitution by the legislatures of three-fourths of the several states within seven years from the date of its submission.

Amendment XXI

December 5, 1933

Section 1. The eighteenth article of amendment to the Constitution of the United States is hereby repealed.

Section 2. The transportation or importation into any state, territory, or possession of the United States for delivery or use therein of intoxicating liquors, in violation of the laws thereof, is hereby prohibited.

Section 3. This article shall be inoperative unless it shall have been ratified as an amendment to the Constitution by conventions in the several states, as provided in the Constitution, within seven years from the date of the submission hereof to the states by the Congress.

Amendment XXII

February 27, 1951

Section 1. No person shall be elected to the office of the President more than twice, and no person who has held the office of President, or acted as President, for more than two years of a term to which some other person was elected President shall be elected to the office of the President more than once. But this article shall not apply to any person holding the office of President when this article was proposed by the Congress, and shall not prevent any person who may be holding the office of President, or acting as President, during the term within which this article becomes operative from holding the office of President or acting as President during the remainder of such term.

Section 2.   This article shall be inoperative unless it shall have been ratified as an amendment to the Constitution by the legislatures of three-fourths of the several states within seven years from the date of its submission to the states by the Congress.

Amendment XXIII

March 29, 1961

Section 1.   The District constituting the seat of government of the United States shall appoint in such manner as the Congress may direct:

A number of electors of President and Vice President equal to the whole number of senators and representatives in Congress to which the district would be entitled if it were a state, but in no event more than the least populous state; they shall be in addition to those appointed by the states, but they shall be considered, for the purposes of the election of President and Vice President, to be electors appointed by a state; and they shall meet in the district and perform such duties as provided by the twelfth article of amendment.

Section 2.   The Congress shall have power to enforce this article by appropriate legislation.

Amendment XXIV

January 23, 1964

Section 1.   The right of citizens of the United States to vote in any primary or other election for President or Vice President, for electors for President or Vice President, or for senator or representative in Congress, shall not be denied or abridged by the United States or any state by reason of failure to pay any poll tax or other tax.

Section 2.   The Congress shall have power to enforce this article by appropriate legislation.

Amendment XXV

February 23, 1967

Section 1.   In case of the removal of the President from office or of his death or resignation, the Vice President shall become President.

Section 2.   Whenever there is a vacancy in the office of the Vice President, the President shall nominate a Vice President who shall take office upon confirmation by a majority vote of both Houses of Congress.

Section 3.   Whenever the President transmits to the President pro tempore of the Senate and the Speaker of the House of Representatives his written declaration that he is unable to discharge the powers and duties of his office, and until he transmits to them a written declaration to the contrary, such powers and duties shall be discharged by the Vice President as Acting President.

Section 4. Whenever the Vice President and a majority of either the principal officers of the executive departments or of such other body as Congress may by law provide, transmit to the President pro tempore of the Senate and the Speaker of the House of Representatives their written declaration that the President is unable to discharge the powers and duties of his office, the Vice President shall immediately assume the powers and duties of the office as acting President.

Thereafter, when the President transmits to the President pro tempore of the Senate and the Speaker of the House of Representatives his written declaration that no inability exists, he shall resume the powers and duties of his office unless the Vice President and a majority of either the principal officers of the executive department or of such other body as Congress may by law provide, transmit within four days to the President pro tempore of the Senate and the Speaker of the House of Representatives their written declaration that the President is unable to discharge the powers and duties of his office. Thereupon Congress shall decide the issue, assembling within forty-eight hours for that purpose if not in session. If the Congress, within twenty-one days after receipt of the latter written declaration, or, if Congress is not in session, within twenty-one days after Congress is required to assemble, determines by two-thirds vote of both Houses that the President is unable to discharge the powers and duties of his office, the Vice President shall continue to discharge the same as acting President; otherwise, the President shall resume the powers and duties of his office.

Amendment XXVI

July 1, 1971

Section 1. The right of citizens of the United States, who are 18 years of age or older, to vote shall not be denied or abridged by the United States or any state on account of age.

Section 2. The Congress shall have the power to enforce this article by appropriate legislation.

Amendment XXVII

May 7, 1992

No law, varying the compensation for the services of the senators and representatives, shall take effect, until an election of representatives shall have intervened.

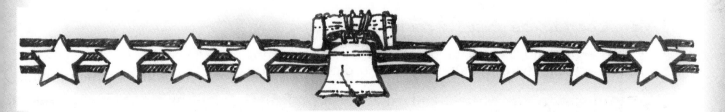

Name _____

Amendments XI Through XXVII Review

Place the amendment number next to the Amendment being described.

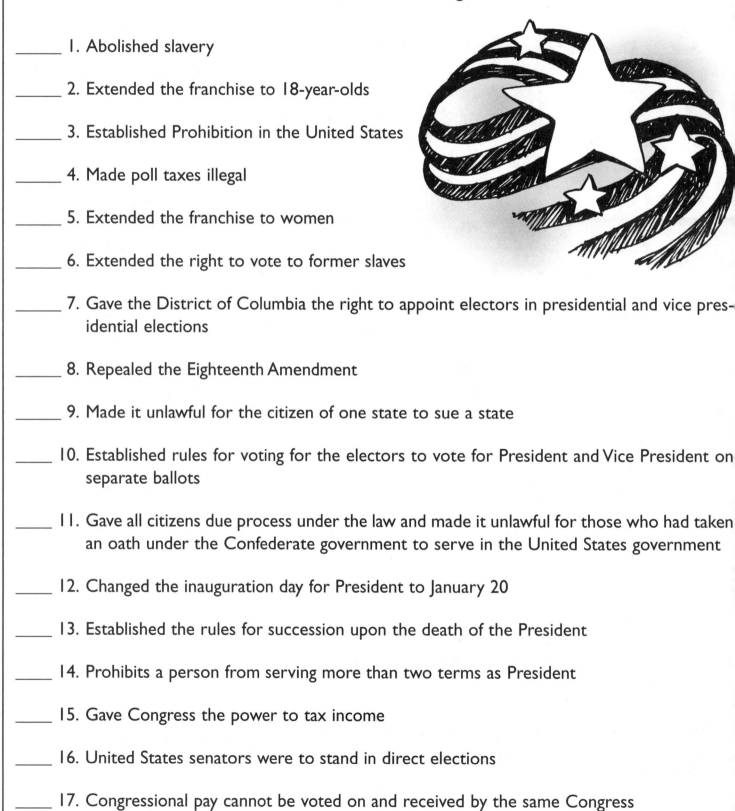

_____ 1. Abolished slavery

_____ 2. Extended the franchise to 18-year-olds

_____ 3. Established Prohibition in the United States

_____ 4. Made poll taxes illegal

_____ 5. Extended the franchise to women

_____ 6. Extended the right to vote to former slaves

_____ 7. Gave the District of Columbia the right to appoint electors in presidential and vice presidential elections

_____ 8. Repealed the Eighteenth Amendment

_____ 9. Made it unlawful for the citizen of one state to sue a state

_____ 10. Established rules for voting for the electors to vote for President and Vice President on separate ballots

_____ 11. Gave all citizens due process under the law and made it unlawful for those who had taken an oath under the Confederate government to serve in the United States government

_____ 12. Changed the inauguration day for President to January 20

_____ 13. Established the rules for succession upon the death of the President

_____ 14. Prohibits a person from serving more than two terms as President

_____ 15. Gave Congress the power to tax income

_____ 16. United States senators were to stand in direct elections

_____ 17. Congressional pay cannot be voted on and received by the same Congress

Name _____

Constitutional or Unconstitutional?

Read the situations below and answer whether you believe the action is constitutional or unconstitutional by circling one. Then explain your answer citing a specific place in the Constitution to support it.

1. The Congress of the United States bestows the title of Princess upon Hannah Montana.

   Constitutional or Unconstitutional?

   Explain your answer. _____

   _____

2. A 20-year-old woman becomes the youngest woman ever elected to the United States Senate from Alaska.

   Constitutional or Unconstitutional?

   Explain your answer. _____

   _____

3. The Senate votes 49 to 52 to ratify a treaty with Peru. The Vice President of the United States casts the 52nd vote in favor of the treaty.

   Constitutional or Unconstitutional?

   Explain your answer. _____

   _____

4. The President of the United States signs an executive order to tax video games at 10% of their purchase price.

   Constitutional or Unconstitutional?

   Explain your answer. _____

   _____

Teacher Notes
Delegates

Delegates to the Constitutional Convention

☆ Indicates delegates who did not sign the Constitution

Contents

56 images—55 portrait cards of the delegates to the Constitutional Convention and William Jackso
the secretary to the Convention.

Bulletin Board Ideas

The images of the delegates can be used to make bulletin boards during the study of the Constitutional Convention. The portrait gallery can be used many ways in the classroom to demonstrate various things about the delegates themselves.

Delegate Map

Create a large map of the states. Separate the delegates by the states they represented at the Constitutional Convention and display each one next to his state.

Invite the students to separate the delegates who did not sign the Constitution by putting a star on each of their portraits.

Graphing

The portrait gallery of the delegates can be use to teach graphing. For instance, invite the stu dents to divide the delegates by age—those i their 20s, those in their 30s, those in the 40s an so forth. Then ask them to create a graph, usin the portraits to make the numbers on the grap for each age level. This process can be used t demonstrate the various occupations.

 # Delegates: What's My Line?

Objective

☆ Students will "teach" each other who the individuals were that signed the Constitution. They will do this by researching the delegates based on the famous painting *The Signing of the Constitution* by Howard C. Christy II. Students will break into teams and ask leading questions to others who are part of the pictorial reenactment.

Background Information

In this challenging game, students will use prior knowledge and deductive reasoning to identify the signers of the Constitution. This game is played similarly to the popular television show *What's My Line?* (A registered trademark of FremantleMedia Operations B.V. Corporation New Zealand Media Centre.)

Group play five or more

Materials

Delegates list and layout, page 142
The Signing of the Constitution painting by Howard C. Christy II,
   page 141
Internet and or reference materials
Markers
Paper and pens

Directions

1. Briefly discuss life in the colonies during the 1700s. Explain how and why a handful of men from various backgrounds, educations and social status chose to represent their states and help develop a Constitution and Bill of Rights for a fledgling country. Review historical information about this period so students understand the depth and importance of the decisions the signers made.

2. Give each player a delegates list and layout, and a copy of the painting *The Signing of the Constitution* by Howard C. Christy II (page 139). Choose one delegate on the layout to highlight. Point out what he looked like as represented in the painting by Howard C. Christy II.

3. Discuss which colony or state the delegate represented, what he did for a living and other biographical facts. Explain to players that they will do their own research for each delegate and document their findings on paper. The facts should include biographical information, place of birth, education and accomplishments. Explain that the information gathered will be used in a game.

4. Allow players to share their newly researched information with other members. Encourage players to take notes to add to their breadth of information on each delegate.

5. Have each player secretly choose one delegate to represent. Three students will act as panelists while one player acts as the delegate. Read the rules at the right and begin play.

Rules

The object of the game is to stump the three panelists as they try to figure out each delegate name. To do this, panelists will play four standard rounds:

a. A round is a guessing game in which the panel tries to identify the delegate by asking a series of questions. The "delegate" may only answer "yes" or "no" when questioned by each panelist.

b. If the answer to the first panelist's question is "yes," the questioning continues.

c. If the "delegates" answer is "no," the second panelist resumes asking questions to discover who the "delegate" is.

d. Panelists have the option of passing on their turn only once. Doing this reveals that they are stumped by who the "delegate" is.

e. Panelists may also request a group conference and openly discuss the exact name of the "delegate."

f. The questions from each panelist continue until the name of the "delegate" is revealed or until the four rounds end.

g. Play continues until all players have had an opportunity to be a panelist and delegate.

The Signing of the Constitution

The Signing of the Constitution Answer Key

1. Washington, George, VA
2. Franklin, Benjamin, PA
3. Madison, James, Jr., VA
4. Hamilton, Alexander, NY
5. Morris, Gouverneur, PA
6. Morris, Robert, PA
7. Wilson, James, PA
8. Pinckney, Charles Cotesworth, SC
9. Pinckney, Charles, SC

11. Butler, Pierce, SC
12. Sherman, Roger, CT
13. Johnson, William Samuel, CT
14. McHenry, James, MD
15. Read, George, DE
16. Bassett, Richard, DE
17. Spaight, Richard Dobbs, NC
18. Blount, William, NC
19. Williamson, Hugh, NC
20. Jenifer, Daniel of St. Thomas, MD

21. King, Rufus, MA
22. Gorham, Nathaniel, MA
23. Dayton, Jonathan, NJ
24. Carroll, Daniel, MD
25. Few, William, GA
26. Baldwin, Abraham, GA
27. Langdon, John, NH
28. Gilman, Nicholas, NH
29. Livingston, William, NJ
30. Paterson, William, NJ

31. Mifflin, Thomas, PA
32. Clymer, George, PA
33. FitzSimons, Thomas, PA
34. Ingersoll, Jared, PA
35. Bedford, Gunning, Jr., DE
36. Brearley, David, NJ
37. Dickinson, John, DE
38. Blair, John, VA
39. Broom, Jacob, DE
40. Jackson, William

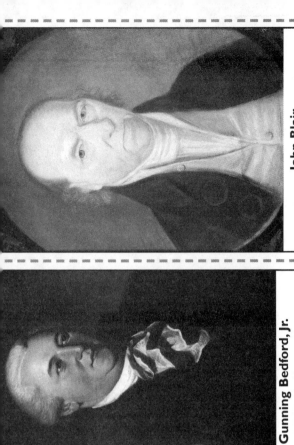

John Blair
(1732-1800), age 55
Virginia
lawyer

Pierce Butler
(1744-1822), age 43
South Carolina
planter
Confederation Congress 1787-1788

Gunning Bedford, Jr.
(1747-1812), age 40
Delaware
lawyer
Confederation Congress 1783-1785

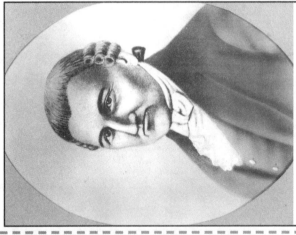

Jacob Broom
(1752-1810), age 35
Delaware
politician, businessman

Richard Bassett
(1745-1815), age 42
Delaware
lawyer

David Brearley
(1745-1790), age 42
New Jersey
lawyer

Abraham Baldwin
(1754-1807), age 33
Georgia
lawyer, minister
Confederation Congress 1785-1786

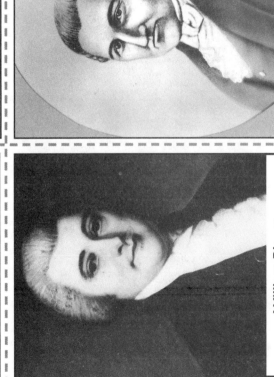

William Blount
(1744-1800), age 43
North Carolina
politician
Confederation Congress
1782-1783, 1786-1788

144

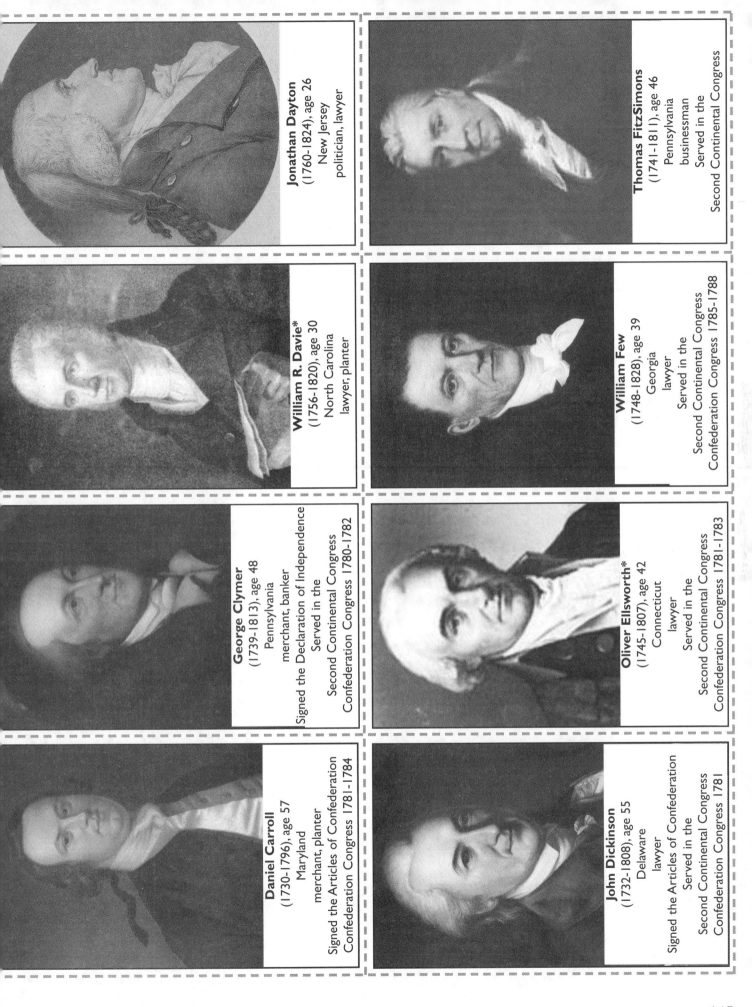

Jonathan Dayton
(1760-1824), age 26
New Jersey
politician, lawyer

Thomas FitzSimons
(1741-1811), age 46
Pennsylvania
businessman
Served in the
Second Continental Congress

William R. Davie*
(1756-1820), age 30
North Carolina
lawyer, planter

William Few
(1748-1828), age 39
Georgia
lawyer
Served in the
Second Continental Congress
Confederation Congress 1785-1788

George Clymer
(1739-1813), age 48
Pennsylvania
merchant, banker
Signed the Declaration of Independence
Served in the
Second Continental Congress
Confederation Congress 1780-1782

Oliver Ellsworth*
(1745-1807), age 42
Connecticut
lawyer
Served in the
Second Continental Congress
Confederation Congress 1781-1783

Daniel Carroll
(1730-1796), age 57
Maryland
merchant, planter
Signed the Articles of Confederation
Confederation Congress 1781-1784

John Dickinson
(1732-1808), age 55
Delaware
lawyer
Signed the Articles of Confederation
Served in the
Second Continental Congress
Confederation Congress 1781

146

Nathaniel Gorham
(1738-1796), age 49
Massachusetts
businessman
Served in the
Second Continental Congress
Confederation Congress
1782-1783, 1785-1787

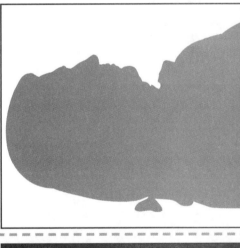

Jared Ingersoll
(1749-1822), age 37
Pennsylvania
lawyer
Served in the
Second Continental Congress

Nicholas Gilman
(1755-1814), age 32
New Hampshire
politician, businessman
Served in the
Second Continental Congress
Confederation Congress 1786-1788

William Houstoun*
(1755-1813), age 32
Georgia
lawyer
Confederation Congress 1784-1785

Elbridge Gerry*
(1744-1814), age 43
Massachusetts
businessman
Signed the Declaration of Independence
Served in the
Second Continental Congress
Confederation Congress 1783-1785

William C. Houston*
(1746-1788), age 41
New Jersey
educator
Served in the
Second Continental Congress
Confederation Congress 1783-1785

Benjamin Franklin
(1706-1790), age 81
Pennsylvania
author, scientist, inventor
Signed the Declaration of Independence
Served in the
Second Continental Congress

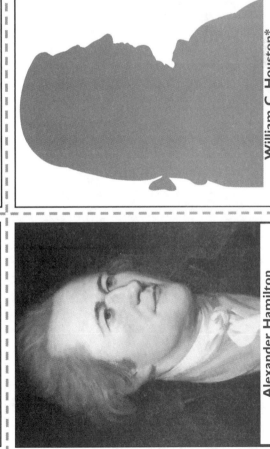

Alexander Hamilton
(1757-1804), age 30
New York
lawyer
Served in the
Second Continental Congress
Confederation Congress 1782-1783

148

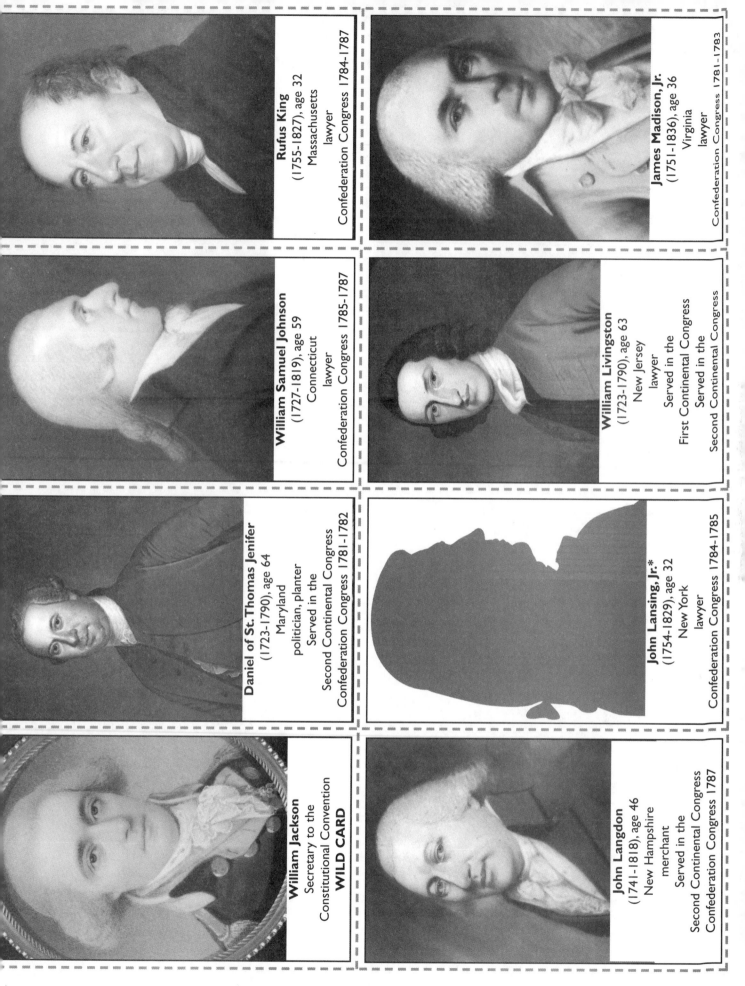

Rufus King
(1755-1827), age 32
Massachusetts
lawyer
Confederation Congress 1784-1787

James Madison, Jr.
(1751-1836), age 36
Virginia
lawyer
Confederation Congress 1781-1783

William Samuel Johnson
(1727-1819), age 59
Connecticut
lawyer
Confederation Congress 1785-1787

William Livingston
(1723-1790), age 63
New Jersey
lawyer
Served in the
First Continental Congress
Served in the
Second Continental Congress

Daniel of St. Thomas Jenifer
(1723-1790), age 64
Maryland
politician, planter
Served in the
Second Continental Congress
Confederation Congress 1781-1782

John Lansing, Jr.*
(1754-1829), age 32
New York
lawyer
Confederation Congress 1784-1785

William Jackson
Secretary to the
Constitutional Convention
WILD CARD

John Langdon
(1741-1818), age 46
New Hampshire
merchant
Served in the
Second Continental Congress
Confederation Congress 1787

150

James McClurg* (1746-1823), age 41
Virginia
physician

George Mason* (1725-1792), age 62
Virginia
politician, planter

Luther Martin* (1748-1826), age 39
Maryland
lawyer

Alexander Martin* (1740-1807), age 47
North Carolina
politician
Confederation Congress 1784-1785

Gouverneur Morris (1752-1816), age 35
Pennsylvania
lawyer
Signed the Articles of Confederation
Served in the
Second Continental Congress

Thomas Mifflin (1744-1800), age 43
Pennsylvania
merchant
Served in the
First Continental Congress
Served in the
Second Continental Congress
Confederation Congress 1782-1784

John F. Mercer* (1759-1821), age 28
Maryland
lawyer
Confederation Congress 1782-1784

James McHenry* (1743-1816), age 44
Maryland
physician
Confederation Congress 1783-1786

152

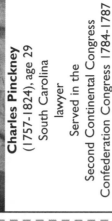

Charles Pinckney
(1757-1824), age 29
South Carolina
lawyer
Served in the
Second Continental Congress
Confederation Congress 1784-1787

John Rutledge
(1739-1800), age 48
South Carolina
lawyer
Served in the
First Continental Congress
Confederation Congress 1782-1783

William L. Pierce*
(1740-1789), age 47
Georgia
merchant
Confederation Congress 1787

George Read
(1733-1798), age 53
lawyer
Delaware
Signed the Declaration of Independence
Served in the
First Continental Congress
Confederation Congress 1782-1783

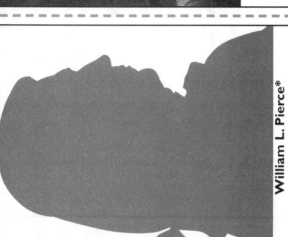

William Paterson (Patterson)
(1745-1806), age 41
New Jersey
lawyer

Edmund J. Randolph*
(1753-1813), age 34
Virginia
planter
Served in the
Second Continental Congress
Confederation Congress 1781-1782

Robert Morris
(1734-1806), age 53
Pennsylvania
merchant
Signed the Declaration of Independence
Signed the Articles of Confederation
Served in the
Second Continental Congress

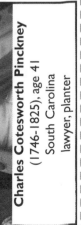

Charles Cotesworth Pinckney
(1746-1825), age 41
South Carolina
lawyer, planter

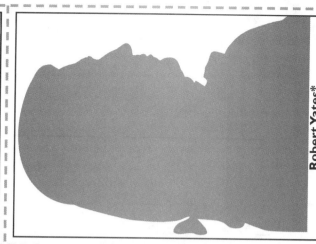

George Washington
(1732-1799), age 55
Virginia
planter, soldier
Served in the
First Continental Congress
Served in the
Second Continental Congress

Robert Yates*
(1738-1801), age 49
New York
lawyer

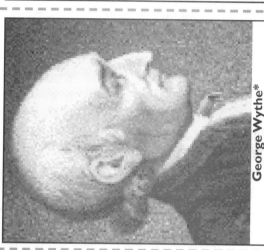

Caleb Strong*
(1745-1819), age 42
Massachusetts
lawyer

George Wythe*
(1726-1806), age 61
Virginia
lawyer
Signed the Declaration of Independence
Served in the
Second Continental Congress

Richard Dobbs Spaight
(1758-1802), age 29
North Carolina
politician
Confederation Congress 1783-1785

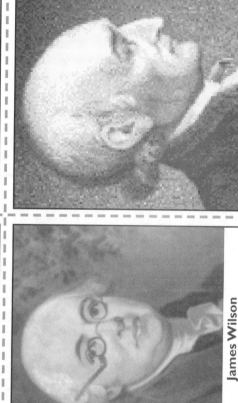

James Wilson
(1742-1798), age 45
Pennsylvania
lawyer
Signed the Declaration of Independence
Served in the
Second Continental Congress
Confederation Congress
1782-1783, 1785-1787

Roger Sherman
(1721-1793), age 66
Connecticut
lawyer; shoe cobbler
Signed the Declaration of Independence
Signed the Articles of Confederation
Served in the
First Continental Congress
Served in the
Second Continental Congress
Confederation Congress 1783-1784

Hugh Williamson
(1735-1819), age 52
North Carolina
physician
Confederation Congress 1782-1785

Rising Sun Plaque and Founding Kids

Objective

☆ Students will make a plaque, replicating the Rising Sun from the original chair that George Washington sat on during the signing of the Constitution. They will then choose a delegate who signed the Constitution and write a brief biography of him. Students will also write their own biographies. The impressions of the student and the Founding Father will be placed side by side on the plaque indicating that people today have the same opportunities and responsibilities to change the world and live up to the true standards of the Constitution. Instead of "Founding Fathers" students become "Founding Kids."

Background Information

This project gives students a taste of the drama, power and significance of those who were bold enough to create our democracy and Constitution. The symbol of this period is best represented in Benjamin Franklin's words while signing the Constitution. During the days of debates, he studied a chair in which the Speaker, George Washington, sat. On the headrest was a painted sun. Franklin reportedly remarked, "I have often looked at that behind the President without being able to tell whether it was rising or setting. But now I . . . know that it is a rising . . . sun."

Reference quote found at http://www.nps.gov/history/museum/exhibits/revwar/image_gal/indeimg/armchair.html

Per one student

Materials

Self-hardening clay
Plastic craft sheets that shrink with heat, found in craft stores
Clear adhesive tape
Cookie sheet
Permanent marker, black fine point
Permanent marker, black thick point
Parchment paper, 8½" x 11"
Cement glue
Scissors
Spray gloss
Light brown varnish
Fine-grade sand paper
White glue

Directions

1. Roll out the self-hardening clay to ¹/₂" thick, with diameter of 11" x 14". Set aside and let dry.

2. Copy the Rising Sun Chair Design (page 150). Tape a clear plastic craft sheet onto the design. Draw the outline of the design with thick black marker. Use the thick black maker to add the interior highlights and lines within the design.

3. Pull the plastic sheet from the design and toss away the tape. Cut the design from the sheet, keeping a ¹/₂" to ¹/₄" border from the thick exterior outline. Place the plastic on a cookie sheet and follow the manufacturer's directions to heat the oven and shrink the plastic. Keep an eye on the heating plastic until it has completely shrunk. Pull it quickly from the oven and immediately place a flat Pyrex™ dish or other flat, heavy object on the sun design so it does not curl. Allow it to set for a while.

4. Choose a favorite delegate from the list in this chapter. Write a short biography on him. Write a personal biography about your own life. Type both biographies and print them on one sheet of parchment paper.

5. Sand the dried clay plaque to make it smooth. Sand the sides as well. Clean off any dust and spray a coat of brown varnish onto the clay, then set aside to dry.

6. Color the back of the shrunk sun design with yellow marker and let dry. Center the sun design at the top of the plaque and glue with plastic adhesive. Center the biographic sheet below the sun design. Allow both to dry. Spray several coats of clear varnish onto the plaque. Allow time to dry between coats.

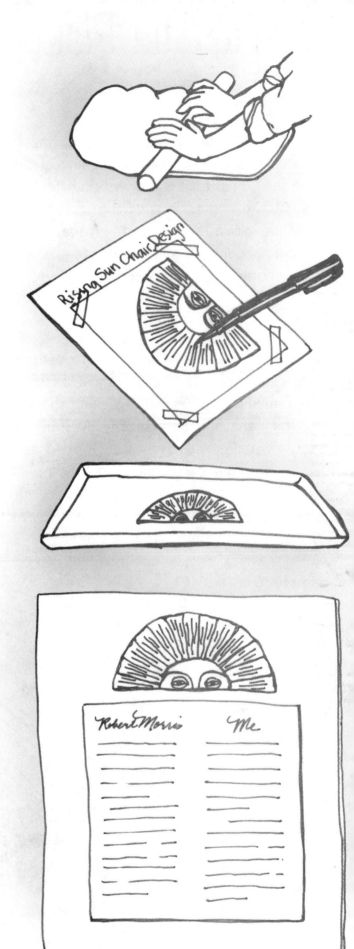

158

Rising Sun Chair Design

Answer Key

Constitutional Time Line, page 9
May 25, 1787: The Constitutional Convention convenes in Philadelphia.
September 17, 1787: The Constitution is approved.
December 7, 1787: Delaware becomes the first state to ratify the Constitution.
June 21, 1788: New Hampshire becomes the ninth state to ratify the Constitution.
April 1, 1789: The United States House of Representatives is organized.
April 30, 1789: George Washington is inaugurated as the first President of the United States.

The Grand Constitution: Or, the Palladium of Columbia: A New Federal Song, pages 15-16
Answers will vary, but may include the following:
1. The beginning stanza describes America as oppressed, credit expiring, commerce distressed. It is a dismal place.
2. The British (This is not in the song.)
3. The song suggests that uniting under the Constitution will save their freedom.
4. The nine muses of mythology
5. Coming home to the farm
6. Riches through global trade
7. The lyricist is using two of the most well-known and beloved Americans as endorsements for ratification of the Constitution.
8. Endorsement (Answers will vary.)
9. They were contemporaries and leaders in the Shays Rebellion.
10. Plenty, order, freedom, independence, culture and payment for toil
11. Glittering generalities (Answers will vary.)
12. In favor (Answers will vary.)

The Preamble, page 24
Definitions will vary.
1. To form a more perfect Union.
2. Establish justice.
3. Insure domestic tranquility.
4. Provide for the common defense.
5. Promote the general welfare.
6. Secure the blessings of liberty for ourselves and our posterity.

The Preamble: "in order to form a more perfect Union, . . ."; page 25
A, D, G, H

The Preamble: "establish justice, . . ."; page 26
A, D, F, G

The Preamble: "insure domestic tranquility, . . ."; page 27
D, F

The Preamble: "provide for the common defense, . . ."; page 28
A, C, D, F, H

The Preamble: "promote the general welfare, . . ."; page 29
A, B, D, F, H

The Preamble: "and secure the blessings of liberty to ourselves and our posterity, . . ."; page 30
A

Senators and Representatives, page 43
1. Must be 25 years old.
   Must have lived in the United States for at least seven years.
   Must live in the state in which elected.
2. Apportioned by the census every 10 years.

3. The governor of the state from which there is a vacancy.
4. Two years
5. Must be at least 30 years old.
   Must be a United States citizen for at least nine years.
   Must be an inhabitant of the state for which he shall be chosen.
6. Vice President of the United States
7. Two

The Senate and the House, page 44
House: B, D, E, G
Senate: A, C, F, H

The President, page 51
1. Must be at least 35 years old.
   Must be a natural born citizen.
   Must have lived the last 14 years in the United States.
2. Executive
3. Vice President
4. Four years
5. I do solemnly swear (or affirm) that I will faithfully execute the office of President of the United States, and will to the best of my ability, preserve, protect and defend the Constitution of the United States.
6. Commander in Chief of the armed forces; shall have the power to grant reprieves and pardons; power to make treaties; power to appoint ambassadors, other public ministers, Supreme Court justices; give the State of the Union Address

2000 Presidential Electoral Map, page 53
Bush: 271
Gore: 266
Nader: 0
Buchanan: 0
Other: 0

Articles III Through VII, pages 67-68
1. Judicial
2. Cases in which the court is where the case is taken to be heard in the first place.
3. All cases affecting ambassadors, public ministers, consuls and those in which a state is a party.
4. The Supreme Court can declare laws unconstitutional.
5. Article III, Section 2, "such trial shall be held in the state where the said crimes shall have been committed; but when not committed within any state, the trial shall be at such place or places as the Congress may by law have directed."
6. Republican form of government
7. 1. ⅔ of both Houses of Congress can propose an amendment.
   2. ⅔ of the State Legislatures can propose an amendment.
8. 1. ¾ of the State Legislatures
   2. Conventions in ¾ of the states
9. United States government
10. nine

Not Allowed—Allowed, page 79
1. The Ten Commandments
2. The heading and 10 numbers
3. United States Supreme Court
4. "Historical Marker"
5. It is a religious symbol. The Constitution guarantees religious freedom, but says the government won't do anything to establish a state religion.
6. Freedom of religion and not establishing a state religion.
7. Answers will vary.

Protecting Democracy . . ., page 81
1. A cafe or a newsroom
2. President George W. Bush

3. Exaggerated ears, smile and caricature of George Bush
4. Two people speaking on talk shows; a peace march; a man reading the newspaper; and a man talking
5. Answers will vary but may include: The man decrying free speech is speaking freely.

The First Amendment (Amended), page 82
First Amendment

The First Amendment (Amended), page 83
1. A news reporter
2. Type
3. In a jail cell
4. Bars on the door windows, chains on his hands.
5. Answers will vary but may include: If people think they can't talk without being anonymous they might not give information to reporters.
6. By limiting freedom of the press and reporters' ability to get a story.
7. Answers will vary but may include: Reporters will not be able to get sources to come forward to tell what they know.

Dissent—As American as . . ., page 84
First Amendment

Dissent—As American as . . ., page 85
1. A sign saying "DISSENT" and an apple pie.
2. The freedom to assemble peacefully and protest.
3. Answers will vary but may include: That protesting is as American and as wholesome as those things we hold dear—such as our mom and her apple pie.
4. Mom and apple pie
5. Answers will vary but may include: Because these two things are recognized as a good part of America.

Getting Signatures for the Petition, page 86
First Amendment

Getting Signatures for the Petition, page 87
1. A petition
2. Sign the petition for a new city government.
3. A throng of people rush to sign the petition.
4. People have the ability and freedom to petition the government when they have a grievance.
5. Answers will vary but may include: Only men could vote before 1920.

"I'm taking a poll, Sir. Are you for or against gun control?" Cartoon, page 97
1. B
2. B
3. B
Bonus: Answers will vary but may include: Most likely this couple opposes gun control since both of them have guns.

"I'd like to stay in your house for a few days with my platoon—we don't eat much." Cartoon, page 99
1. B
2. A
3. C
Bonus: Before and during the American Revolution, British soldiers were often quartered or housed in private homes.

NSA Cartoon, page 101
1. C
2. B
3. C
4. A

"All right, Spottie, bark once for 'yes,' and twice for 'no' and five times if you wish to take the 5th." Cartoon, page 1[0]
1. B
2. A
3. A, B or C
Bonus: Answers will vary but may includ[e] The Fifth Amend-ment guarantees that a person does not have to testify or incrim[i]nate himself. Answer A or B may also be correct since the judge is giving the dog many directions.

"Oh-oh—I should have gone for a jur[y] trial." Cartoon, page 105
1. C
2. A or B
3. C

"If that doesn't work, there is always the People's Court on TV!" Cartoon, page 107
1. C
2. B
3. B

"I sentence you to listening to one hour of Barry Manilow's greatest hits[,] page 109
1. A
2. C
Bonus: Answers will vary but may inclu[de] Being put in a stockade, whipped, dunke[d] etc.

"This is none of your business." page 111
1. B
2. A
3. A

"Stay out of our schools with your rules!" page 113
1. C   2. B
3. C   4. A

Rights Review, page 114
1. 6   2. 6
3. 1   4. 5
5. 6   6. 1
7. 7   8. 8
9. 2   10. 4

Rights Review, page 115
1. 6   2. 1
3. 8   4. 6
5. 3   6. 5
7. 1   8. 6
9. 5   10. 1

Rights Review, page 116
1. • Freedom of religion
   • Freedom of speech
   • Freedom of the press
   • Freedom to assemble
   • Freedom to petition the governme[nt]
2. • Cannot go to trial without a grand jury indictment.
   • Cannot be tried for the same offe[nse] twice.
   • Cannot be compelled to testify ag[ainst] oneself.
   • Cannot be deprived of life, liberty [or] property without due process of [law]
   • Private property cannot be taken [for] public use without just compensat[ion]
3. • No excessive bail
   • No excessive fines
   • No cruel or unusual punishment

Amendments II Through XXVII Review, page 136
1. 13   2. 26
3. 18   4. 24
5. 19   6. 15
7. 23   8. 21
9. 11   10. 12
11. 14   12. 20
13. 25   14. 22
15. 16   16. 17
17. 27

TLC10541 Copyright © Teaching & Learning Company, Carthage, IL 62321-